HAMILTON VERSUS WALL STREET

The Core Principles of the American
System of Economics

NANCY BRADEEN SPANNAUS

HAMILTON VERSUS WALL STREET
THE CORE PRINCIPLES OF THE
AMERICAN SYSTEM OF ECONOMICS

iUniverse books may be ordered through booksellers or by contacting:

iUniverse
1663 Liberty Drive
Bloomington, IN 47403
www.iuniverse.com
1-800-Authors (1-800-288-4677)

ISBN: 978-1-5320-6754-9 (sc)
ISBN: 978-1-5320-6755-6 (e)

Library of Congress Control Number: 2019901442

Print information available on the last page.

iUniverse rev. date: 02/16/2019

CONTENTS

Special thanks to Stuart Rosenblatt; Rand Scholet, founder of the Alexander Hamilton Awareness Society; Jeffrey Steinberg; and my dear husband Ed, for reading my manuscript and providing their insights and encouragement.

Alexander Hamilton as President-General of the Society of the Cincinnati. The painting was done by an unknown artist in the early 19th century, using portraits by John Trumbull. It was lent for exhibition at the Society's headquarters in Washington, D.C. by Mrs. Laurens Hamilton, and photographed by the author. (courtesy of Nancy Spannaus)

INTRODUCTION

*To cherish and stimulate the activity of the human
mind, by multiplying the objects of enterprise, is not
among the least considerable of the expedients, by
which the wealth of a nation may be promoted.*

−Report on Manufactures

THE PURPOSE OF this book is simple: to establish
once and for all that the first U.S. Treasury Secretary,
Alexander Hamilton, was the founder of an American
System of Economics which provided the unique
basis for building the United States into an industrial
powerhouse. Since the popularity of the *Hamilton*
musical has excited a surge of interest in this Founding
Father, we now have a golden opportunity for making
his true ideas broadly known for the first time since the
mid-Nineteenth Century. That opportunity must not
be squandered.

This book is based on my 40 years of study of
Hamilton's ideas and policies on political economy, the
science of building a thriving national economy. My
appreciation of Hamilton's economic vision was first
piqued by my reading of his *Report on Manufactures*; I
was particularly struck by the sentence quoted above.

My further study has led me to conclusions which clash with those of even some of the most pro-Hamilton voices in the country today. I have called for a public debate on Hamilton's economics and their applicability to today, but that has yet to occur. It is my hope that this book will aid in provoking that debate, and the adoption of the Hamiltonian ideas so desperately needed in the United States, and worldwide.

I originally intended this book to be a thorough scholarly treatment of Alexander Hamilton's life and work. Over recent years I read Hamilton's entire collected works with the aim of producing the definitive, in-depth evaluation of his thought.

But that would be a years-long project, and the current opportunity must be seized. So instead, I will present a series of propositions dealing with the core principles Hamilton represents—principles which refute some of the most misleading assertions about his policies–and how they have shaped American and world history. I will start with one of the most dangerous lies of all—that Alexander Hamilton is the father of Wall Street and the financial premises and methods which characterize it today.[1]

---

[1] Critics of Hamilton, from his contemporaries to historian Charles Beard and writers like William Hogeland today, assert this directly. But, as I have observed in many events, many Hamilton lovers implicitly agree. Thus one finds one of the strongest cheering sections for Hamilton among the New York banking crowd and the neo-conservatives (cf. the Alexander Hamilton Society), who ignore his actual revolutionary economic principles.

I begin with a brief profile of Alexander Hamilton, the man. For a man's ideas can never be totally separated from his character.

A Revolutionary Genius

Who was Alexander Hamilton? He was, first and foremost, a revolutionary visionary, who devoted nearly his entire life to creating a new kind of political-economic system uniquely suited to uplifting mankind. His legendary energy, his towering intellect, and even his super-sensitive attention to defending his honor were all vectored toward achieving that primary objective. As George Washington said of Hamilton in a letter to John Adams in 1798, "By some he is considered as an ambitious man, and therefore a dangerous one. That he is ambitious I shall readily grant, but it is of that laudable kind which prompts a man to excel in whatever he takes in hand."

The experiences of Hamilton's early life as an orphan on St. Croix taught him that he had to rely on his intellect to achieve his purposes in life. It also gave him invaluable experience in dealing with international commerce, a step toward seeing himself on the international stage. Fortunately, the individuals who befriended and protected him—from his cousin Ann Lytton Venton[2] and the Rev. Hugh Knox, to the New

---

[2] See "The Woman Who Paid for Alexander Hamilton's Education," by Michael E. Newton, on the Discovering Hamilton blog.

Jersey revolutionary circles around Elias Boudinot[3] and William Livingston—provided support for his voracious studies of history, philosophy, and economy, while bringing him to the American mainland. By 1774, when British oppression in Boston was leading to a revolt against London throughout the colonies, the young Alexander had chosen the revolutionary path, and put his pen to work on its behalf.

The evidence for this is available in Hamilton's extensive 1775 tract known as *The Farmer Refuted*, his second refutation of the attacks on the first Continental Congress by the Tory Rev. Samuel Seabury. This extraordinary document starts from first principles which I believe Hamilton never abandoned, both in terms of Natural Law and economy. The 17-year-old Hamilton, then still at King's College (later Columbia University), already shows intimate familiarity with both English history and the philosophy of law, and he argues systematically from certain fundamental axioms. Among those are these two memorable assertions. The first is that the "*supreme law* of every society" is "*its own happiness*," a view he contrasted with the Hobbesian ("might makes right") view of Rev. Seabury. The second is more well-known:

---

[3] Elias Boudinot was a prominent lawyer and Revolutionary patriot in New Jersey by the time Hamilton arrived. He had close family connections with Benjamin Franklin, and was a trusted collaborator of General Washington during the Revolutionary War. He served both in the Confederation and the U.S. House of Representatives.

The sacred rights of mankind are not to be rummaged for among old parchments or musty records. They are written, as with a sunbeam, in the whole volume of human nature, by the Hand of the Divinity itself, and can never be erased or obscured by mortal power.

Many have argued that, as a result of his experience with treachery among both his allies and his enemies, Hamilton abandoned this "idealistic" outlook. Certainly he did not have a pollyannish view of human nature; he believed that institutions had to be created which would channel men's behavior for the good of society, rather than leaving it to individuals to exercise their individual rights without constraint. But Hamilton remained, despite all his disappointments, a religious man with a commitment to republicanism.

In a letter to his friend Edward Carrington on May 26, 1792, Hamilton responded to charges that he was leading a party seeking monarchy thus: I am "*affectionately* tied to the Republican theory. I desire above all things to see the *quality* of political rights exclusive of all *hereditary* distinction firmly established by a practical demonstration of its being consistent with the order and happiness of society." [emphasis in the original]

I don't believe Hamilton ever abandoned his belief that mankind was imbued with God-given powers. His call for a Christian Constitutionalist Society in the 1800s buttresses my view. Indeed, Hamilton's economic system depends upon the God-given inventive power of the human individual, for the creation of the technological advances upon which human scientific and moral progress depend.

Hamilton is well-known to have shown no interest in personal wealth, and to have been generous to the poor and troubled. His stance against African slavery,[4] and his actions for the education and emancipation of slaves and Native Americans,[5] testify to his commitment to the belief that all men are created equal. Notably, although the 1783 Treaty of Paris called for the British to remunerate American slave-holders for their freed slaves, Hamilton told John Jay, who had negotiated the Treaty, that this plank could be ignored; it was immoral. He also argued that <u>view</u> publicly in his *Camillus* letters in defense of the Jay Treaty, which said nothing about the compensation issue.

Hamilton hated oppression, British or otherwise. He believed in the triumph of reason and truth; just look at his masterful argument for *truth* as the standard

---

[4] Alexander Hamilton was an active member of the New York Manumission Society, which was founded in 1785, and lobbied for emancipation, albeit gradual. His economic system was also antithetical to the slave system.

[5] The Manumission Society established an African Free School in 1787. It was dedicated to teaching black children for a life outside slavery. It ultimately had seven buildings and educated thousands of students. In 1794, Hamilton also became a trustee to the Hamilton-Oneida Academy, an institution dedicated to educating Native Americans.

in libel law in the _Croswell_ case.[6] He was willing to give his life to save the Union which he had helped to create as a bulwark against British or other European destruction of the fledgling United States—and he did.

THE WAR EXPERIENCE

It is impossible to understand Hamilton's principles of political economy without taking his war experience into account. He saw action in the Revolutionary War, from its start in 1774 through the decisive Battle of Yorktown in 1781. He began on the front lines in New York City, where he caught the attention of General Washington for his daring exploits as an artillery captain. Even after he became Washington's chief aide-de-camp in 1777, he was often on the battlefield. He engaged in the Battle of Trenton, at Princeton, and at Monmouth. He suffered with the rest of the army at Valley Forge and Morristown.

Hamilton also saw the war from the standpoint of high command, especially concerning the devastating lack of provisions from the Congress, but also the difficulties in maintaining alliances, and attempting to negotiate prisoner exchanges and other arrangements

---

[6] Hamilton argued the appeal of a conviction of newspaper editor Harry Croswell, who had been convicted of criminal defamation of President Thomas Jefferson. Hamilton argued that the truth of the defamation could be exculpatory if the publication was not done with malicious intent. Under British law, truth was irrelevant, or even made the crime worse.

with the British. As Washington's aide-de-camp, Hamilton took part in strategic planning, and had a sensuous grasp of how the shortfalls in material resources, as well as in human commitment, constantly threatened the revolutionary cause.

Thus, Hamilton's war experience strengthened his identification as an American, not the citizen of any particular state, and as a staunch patriot.

The ties Hamilton formed during the War of Independence led to life-long friendships. He was a prominent member of the Society of the Cincinnati,[7] and continued to be addressed according to his military rank during much of his public life. While he campaigned vigorously for war veterans to be compensated, he himself gave up his claim to a pension upon leaving the Army in 1782. Many of his close associates during the war, such as Gen. Henry Knox, George Washington, the painter John Trumbull, New York City Mayor Richard Varick, and later Secretary of Defense James McHenry, continued to be his collaborators.

Through his war experience, Hamilton got a clear understanding of the mindset and treachery of the British enemy, which was determined, even after a military victory over the Americans was clearly impossible, to defeat the Revolution. British tactics would involve

---

[7] The Society of the Cincinnati was founded by American and French officers in 1783, "to promote knowledge and appreciation of the achievements of the American Revolution" and to promote fellowship among its members, including financial support. Click here for more.

financial warfare, trade embargos, bribing and arming Native Americans to harass the frontier, and even providing funds to distressed American citizens to riot against the government (cf. Shay's Rebellion)[8]. Hamilton knew this, and that the only way the gains of the war could be protected would be to form a strong union, with a constantly improving economic base.

How does Hamilton's revolutionary war experience cohere with the oft-repeated assertion that he (and his close colleague George Washington) sought to use the Constitution to impose British policies on the victorious United States population? *It doesn't*, because Hamilton never sought to do any such thing.

ON TO THE AMERICAN SYSTEM

None of this is to say that Alexander Hamilton did not make mistakes and compromises, and commit irrational acts. Whole books have been devoted to describing them, while virtually burying his accomplishments. Hamilton did not perfectly adhere to the principles he espoused. But it is beyond question that he supplied the spark of revolutionary genius–the ideas, combined with nearly unbelievable energy–that were crucial in creating the United States Republic, and its unique and

---

[8] Historian Forrest McDonald has documented that the British, through Tory doctors, were paying Shays' men 3 shillings a day during their revolt. See *E Pluribus Unum: the formation of the American Republic*, 1776-1790, Liberty Fund, 1965.

successful, but now nearly abandoned American System of political economy.

That American System is the very antithesis of the British imperial system of economy which the American Revolution was fought against, a system which is based on a degraded notion of mankind as a variety of animal, animated by narrow passions, and thus fated to be ruled by an allegedly superior class, i.e., the nobility. The British System has presided over the most horrendous exploitation of mankind (just see the cases of India and Africa), while allowing a financial elite to accumulate untold wealth and power. It lives on today in the world of supranational financial institutions, including the mega-banks on Wall Street, which sacrifice human lives to financial profit all around the world.

For this reason, Alexander Hamilton's principles of political economy must be understood and revived today.

Alexander Hamilton's statue outside the Treasury Department in Washington, D.C. This statue by James Fraser was erected in 1923.

CHAPTER I

Alexander Hamilton would have been the foremost opponent of Wall Street today

The intrinsic wealth of a nation is to be measured, not by the abundance of the precious metals, contained in it, but by the quantity of the productions of its labor and industry.

—Report on a National Bank

ALMOST EVERY BIOGRAPHY of Alexander Hamilton, contemporary or historical, will tell you—explicitly or implicitly—that he was the Father of Wall Street, meaning the corrupt system of financial markets dominated by the mega-banks which we have today. That assertion is the basis for either the most passionate love or most intense hatred of our first Secretary of the Treasury. But what if that assertion is not true?

It *is* true that Hamilton set up the system of government securities (bonds) which became the object of the private financial markets, and that New York City's Wall Street area was a major center for these markets. He also established the First Bank of the United States (in Philadelphia), which utilized those bonds as capital, and proceeded to play a critical role in moving toward a uniform national currency for the nation. This was the *sine qua non* for establishing the sovereign power of the national government. The result of these measures was to raise the credit worthiness of the United States government, and the ability for merchants, tradesmen, and farmers alike to carry on profitable commerce, and develop the country's productive base.

From the beginning, Hamilton's financial system was under attack. Some of those attacks even came from his nominal allies, who opposed his vision to turn the United States into an industrial republic. They were, quite literally, in it for the money.

But Hamilton himself was clear that his purpose in establishing these "financial instruments" was the exact opposite of the purposes of financial speculators and usurers, the likes of whom have dominated Wall Street for many extended periods in American history. Hamilton intended that his financial system be managed for building up the physical economy of the nation, the real source of wealth and prosperity. Through his system, the wealthy were to be encouraged to invest in that process of developing the nation; private profit and profit for the nation were to be wedded.

Land should be developed, interest rates should be reasonable, and banking should be vectored toward increasing the productive powers of labor in agriculture and manufacturing. Such conditions were, in fact, the prerequisite for a stable, solvent, unified government.

Thus, Hamilton's watchword was credit, public credit. Credit is the basis for investing for future returns, for making the economy more profitable in the long term. For a nation to do that requires leadership that understands how a physical economy increases its productivity, and which creates a system that fosters investments that do just that. Hamilton's passion was to build a nation that would so prosper. Historian Forrest McDonald showed an understanding of this purpose when he wrote

> What was important was that there would be a banking system, and that the currency of the nation would be based upon it, not upon gold and silver. That meant the nation could be built on credit, for the crucial characteristic of banking currency is that it is money created in the present, not out of past savings but out of the expectation of future profits.[1]

---

[1] Forrest McDonald, *Alexander Hamilton, A Biography*, W.W. Norton & Company, New York, 1979.

WHAT'S THE MATTER WITH WALL STREET?

Just how did Hamilton's vision differ from that of the major banks in that area of Manhattan called Wall Street? After all, Hamilton himself founded the Bank of New York, which was a major financial player, and still exists today. Certainly, some would argue, these bankers played some positive role in building the wealth of the nation.

Unfortunately, the record shows that through most of its history, the Wall Street banks played a negative role, choosing to use their funds for speculation rather than building the economy, gouging the public with usurious interest rates, and even actively opposing the Federal government on vital matters of national and economic security. It was Wall Street bankers, often serving as junior partners to London banking, who supported the slave system, who carried out virtual extortion against the Lincoln Administration (see chapter 5), and who sought to stymie Franklin Roosevelt's plans to get out of the Great Depression (see chapter 6).

The Wall Street mindset can fairly be described as geared toward short-term financial gain *per se*, rather than actual economic growth. Some of the most flagrant examples have occurred in recent decades, as in the leveraged buyouts of major production companies, which resulted in loading those companies with debt, and then drastically downsizing or even closing the company (cf. the RJR Nabisco case in 1988). Another case-in-point was the hedge fund Trian's forcing of DuPont to lay off 5000 workers in 2015, including 1700 from their R&D lab—all in the interest of driving up the share price. (It went up 210%!)

In the same category is the much-discussed Wall Street practice of lending money to companies to buy back their own stock, instead of re-investing in the business; the extraordinary profits being made by the major Wall Street banks by borrowing money cheaply from the Fed and lending at exorbitant rates; and the extraordinary decline in the percentage of bank lending actually going into long-term physical investment as opposed to takeovers, mergers, and other financial maneuvers.[2]

From Hamilton's standpoint, today's stock-market bubbles—built through gambling bets on derivatives, corporate buybacks of their own stock, and other purely financial games—would have been anathema. The same with the issuance of fiat money by the Federal Reserve to support the major financial institutions on Wall Street, and to keep the markets churning, while desperately needed infrastructure projects and worthy industries are unable to find the affordable credit to invest and grow. Instead of finance being the instrument

---

[2] One very useful chronicling of this process of starving the physical economy in favor of financial rip-offs can be found in the book *Makers and Takers, The Rise of Finance and the Fall of Business* by Rana Foroohar, published in 2016. A review can be found at https://americansystemnow.

for building the nation through industry, industry has been "financialized" to a disastrous degree.

Crucial evidence for Hamilton's outlook exists both in his writings, especially his *Second Report on Public Credit* (*Report on a National Bank*), and in the actions he took to defuse the great speculative boom in 1791-1792.

FROM THE REPORT ON A NATIONAL BANK

Hamilton's arguments in favor of a National Bank reflect his view of the function of banks in general. He was well aware of the role that British banking had played in oppressing the American colonists prior to the Constitution, especially through usury and the restriction of credit.[3] That British stranglehold on credit—codified in the Currency Act of 1764, which demanded that the colonies exchange their scrip for Bank of England notes—had a devastating impact on American commerce. Benjamin Franklin has been quoted saying that "In one year the conditions were so reversed that the era of prosperity ended, and a depression set in, to such an extent that the streets of the Colonies were filled with the unemployed."

---

[3] Understanding that the growth of their economies depended upon the extension of credit, many colonies, especially Massachusetts and Pennsylvania, had developed a system of paper currency independent of their British colonial masters. This is what the Crown moved to crush, in its attempt to prevent American industrialization.

Thus, Hamilton had his work cut out for him. He had to confront the national prejudice against banking as it was being practiced by the British, by showing the advantages of a well-run National Bank.

In his Second Report on Public Credit (*Report on a National Bank*), issued December 13, 1790, Hamilton began by citing the principal advantages of a Bank: "the augmentation of the active or productive capital of a country," turning "dead stock" (money or assets sitting idle, including gold and silver) into the basis for a "paper circulation" which permits the expansion of wealth. The money in a bank will thus become credit for trade and industry, rather than lying idle. In sum, "by contributing to enlarge the mass of industrious and commercial enterprise, banks become nurseries of national wealth: a consequence, as satisfactorily verified by experience, as it is clearly deducible in theory."

Conversely, any bank which does not provide credit for expanding industry and commerce, is not acting in the public interest. Indeed, the fact that corporate charters are granted to banking institutions by government bodies underscores the fact that they have a fiduciary responsibility to the public, not just to their boards of directors and executives. Just the antithesis of Wall Street's practice today.

Implicitly addressing the malfeasance by the British financial institutions which had immiserated his fellow Americans, Hamilton then turned to dealing with the arguments against banks *per se*, specifically:

- That they serve to increase usury;
- That they tend to prevent other kinds of lending;
- That they furnish temptations to overtrading;
- That they afford aid to ignorant adventurers who disturb the natural and beneficial course of trade;
- That they give to bankrupt and fraudulent traders a fictitious credit…; and lastly
- That they tend to banish gold and silver from the country.

The first and last of these are the most pertinent to our argument.

After some remarks about how desperation for money causes people to resort to usurers, Hamilton puts forward a

> leading view, in which the tendency of banks will be seen to be, to abrige [sic] rather than to promote usury. This relates to their property of increasing the quantity and quickening the circulation of money. If it be evidence, that usury will prevail or diminish, according to the proportion which the demand for borrowing bears to the quantity of money at market to be lent; whatever has the property just mentioned, whether it be in the shape of paper or of coin, by contributing to render the supply

> more equal to the demand, must tend
> to counteract the progress of usury.

By providing more plentiful credit, Hamilton's bank would work against usury. In fact, Hamilton's Bank proposal called for a limitation of interest charges to six percent, and his reorganization of the national debt, the subject of his *First Report on Public Credit*, actually reduced the operative interest rates on that debt.[4] In effect, he told the nation's creditors that they could either accept lower interest paid regularly on a secure investment in long-term government bonds, or demand higher rates for which they could wait forever.

Hamilton minimizes the dangers of the next objections, noting that "there is scarcely a source of public prosperity, which will not be speedily ... closed," if one judges by whether that source has ever been abused. The evil must be weighed against the good, and "in the present case such a comparison will issue in this, that the new and increased energies derived to commercial enterprise, from the aid of banks, are a source of general profit and advantage; which greatly outweigh the partial ills of the overtrading of a few individuals, at particular times, or of numbers in particular conjunctures."

He then turns to what he calls the "heaviest charge" against his Bank proposal: the assertion that banks

---

[4] Donald F. Swanson, "Origins of Hamilton's Fiscal Policies," University of Florida Monographs, *Social Sciences*, no. 17, winter 1963.

tend to banish the silver and gold of a country. The fundamental, although "not intirely [sic] satisfactory," answer to this charge is *that the intrinsic wealth of a nation is to be measured, not by the abundance of the precious metals, contained in it, but by the quantity of the productions of its labor and industry.* Hamilton's own treatment of money and coinage indicate that he did not believe that gold and silver had intrinsic value; rather, their value was in their ability to provide a stable medium for productive activity, stability, and the security of property in the nation.

Hamilton goes on to say that of course it is not a matter of indifference as to whether a nation has access to specie; but it is "the state of its [a nation's] agriculture and manufactures, the quantity and *quality* of its labor and industry" which determines whether it has access to those precious metals [emphasis in the original].

Therefore, in this seminal document, Hamilton has laid out arguments which show that his view of the principles and standards of sound banking are totally the opposite of those practiced by Wall Street today: A bank's function is to promote active capital in agriculture and manufactures, increasing the quantity and quality of labor and industry. They are credit institutions, created to invest in creating productive wealth, not just producing more financial profit. He even adds explicitly that

> *Public utility is more truly the object of public Banks, than private profit. And it is the*

business of Government, to constitute them on such principles, that while the latter will result, to a significant degree, to afford competent motives to engage in them, the former be not made subservient to it.

An etching of the Burr-Hamilton duel in July 1804, which proved fatal to Hamilton. At that time, and later, Burr was acting as an agent of British enemies of Hamilton's system and the United States as a whole.

HAMILTON'S WAR AGAINST THE SPECULATORS

Critics of Hamilton argue that his actions as Secretary of the Treasury betrayed a desire to pander to the rich, no matter what his stated intentions were. While there were obviously "bad apples" who made their way into

Hamilton's confidence (cf. William Duer[5]) and did temporary damage, the Treasury Secretary's actions in the 1791–1792 speculative bubble demonstrate his clear determination to squash the speculative class.

From the very start of the Bank of the United States (BUS) in the Summer of 1791, it was the target of attack by speculative financial interests. Stock prices were bid up from $25 a share to $300 in the four weeks after the BUS opened for business, only to crash back down to $110 a share a couple weeks later. Recognizing this action as a danger to the stabilization of credit, Hamilton prevailed upon his friends at the Bank of New York (which he had helped to found in 1784) to intervene.

However, a few months later, what Hamilton considered "bancomania" broke out again, spurred by speculators organized around Hamilton's friend and former Treasury official Duer. Another bubble in bank stocks erupted during the Winter of 1791–1792, buttressed by the decision of Hamilton's political foes to establish three new banking institutions, which were immediately massively oversubscribed. In essence, a bank war had broken out, as the new institutions sought to topple and/or take over the Bank of New

---

[5] William Duer was a New York lawyer and businessman who joined the Revolutionary cause in 1775. He served in the New York State Senate, the Continental Congress, and as Assistant Secretary of the Treasury. Hamilton fired him from the Treasury after 7 months, upon indications of his impropriety.

York, which was working in close collaboration with the BUS.

Hamilton denounced this speculative mania in the following terms:

"These extravagant sallies of speculation do injury to the government and to the whole system of public credit by disgusting all sober citizens and giving a wild air to everything.... The superstructure of credit is now too vast for the foundation. It must be gradually brought within more reasonable dimensions or it will tumble." He added that such "banking activity" reflected "a spirit of gambling."

To stem the panic, Hamilton had to take legal action against the main instigator, his friend Duer, as well as getting the Bank of New York to purchase a large amount of government securities to stabilize the price. Although he could not relieve the pain of the hundreds of citizens who had gambled with Duer, and now found the value of their purchases crashing down, Hamilton acted to bring stability back to the market. "There should be a line of separation between honest men and knaves, between respectable stockholders and dealers in the funds and mere unprincipled gamblers," Hamilton wrote. "Public infamy must restrain what the laws cannot."

The foregoing should make clear that Hamilton stood staunchly against Wall Street speculation, unlike the group of financiers who formed themselves as the Buttonwood Club in the Spring of 1792, and eventually formed the New York Stock Exchange. His interest was in ensuring that the financial markets provided a stable basis for government credit and for investment in industry and commerce, and not in providing the means for individuals to get rich off arbitrage and mere trading of shares. Indeed, Wall Street today is the descendant of Hamilton's enemies in 1791–1792.

THE MANHATTAN COMPANY—'A PERFECT MONSTER'

The genesis of Chase Manhattan Bank (today's JPMorgan Chase) provides a striking example of the difference between Hamilton's concept of banking and that of his financial adversaries on Wall Street. In 1798, New York City, like other cities in the nation, was ravaged by a Yellow Fever epidemic. The devastation called attention to the state of the City's water supply and system, which was dependent upon often-polluted wells and thus was held in part responsible for the spread of the disease. In response, two proposals were brought before the City's Common Council—one for a public water system and the other for a private system; both would bring fresh water from the Bronx River.[6]

Behind the plan for the private system was none other than Aaron Burr, at that time a prominent representative of Thomas Jefferson's Democratic-Republican Party in

---

[6] A detailed description of the circumstances around the founding of the Bank of Manhattan can be found in Ron Chernow's *Hamilton* biography.

the state. Burr solicited the support of leading Federalists, including Hamilton, for his plan for a "water company"; with this political leverage (the Federalists being in control of the New York State Assembly at the time), the Manhattan Company was able to gain a charter from the state in April-May of 1799. The Company's elaborate plans for a new city water system, including installing sewers, draining swamps, and providing the new clean water source, had been drafted by Alexander Hamilton himself.

But Burr had no intention of using the new company to improve the City's water system. His aim was to use it as a ploy to authorize the establishment of a new bank, to compete with the Bank of New York and the New York City branch of the Bank of the United States. To this end, he included in the fine print the following language: "that it shall and may be lawful for the said company to employ all such surplus capital as may belong or accrue to the said company in the purchase of public or other stock or in any other monied transactions of operations." The unsuspecting Federalists failed to notice until it was too late, and the charter had been approved by the New York State Assembly.

By no later than September of 1799, the ruse was fully exposed when the Manhattan Company opened an "office of discount and deposit" on Wall Street and commenced operations as the bank Burr had intended. The bank then proceeded to issue loans to the benefit of the Democratic-Republican Party, as well as its financiers.

The plans for a new system of waterworks from an unpolluted source were discarded.

In an 1801 letter to Sen. James Bayard during the stalemate between Burr and Jefferson for the Presidency, Hamilton used the incident as an example of Burr's character: *"He has lately by a trick established a bank, a perfect monster in its principles, but a very convenient instrument of profit and influence."*

Those principles, as shown in action, were to eschew investment in the physical health and welfare of the population; to lie, cheat, and steal in favor of personal profit. Those are the principles which have in fact characterized the successors of the Manhattan Company—the Manhattan Bank, the Chase Manhattan Bank, and now JPMorgan Chase—to this very day. No wonder it is JPMorgan Chase which holds title to the very pistols used in the Burr-Hamilton duel.

I have no doubt that, if Hamilton had a chance, he would use his system to crush such major Wall Street speculators today.

Tobacco.

Industry, or Slavery? Cotton Mills, using the most advanced technology of the time, represented the onset of an industrial America. The mill shown here was operated in Paterson, New Jersey, home of Hamilton's SUM. It is pictured in the Paterson Museum. (photo courtesy of Nancy Spannaus) Meanwhile much of the country still clung to slave labor. Shown here are slaves working on a tobacco plantation.

CHAPTER 2

Hamilton's *Report on Manufactures* is the Rosetta Stone[1] of his thinking on economics.

Manufacturing establishments not only occasion a positive augmentation of the Produce and Revenue of the Society, but that they contribute essentially to rendering them greater than they could possibly be, without such establishments.

—Report on Manufactures

IF YOU WANT to understand a person's behavior or thought, you must first understand where he or she is

---

[1] The Rosetta Stone was a stone slab (stele) discovered in 1799 in Egypt, which provided the key to deciphering previously unintelligible Egyptian hieroglyphics. It has come to be a metaphor for a tool that clarifies the meaning of difficult or complex texts.

intending to go, or what he or she wants to achieve. Thus, the key to understanding Alexander Hamilton's financial system lies in the document which lays out his vision for the nation in the broadest scope, his 1791 *Report on the Subject of Manufactures.* It is only by understanding that broad vision, not by a process of induction from the detailed steps which he laid out to get there, that you can adduce the principles of the American System of political economy which Hamilton founded.

The *Report on Manufactures* was Hamilton's fourth major state paper, submitted on December 5, 1791 in response to a January 15, 1790 order from the House of Representatives, and the wishes of President Washington. Hamilton had been explicitly commissioned to provide a plan "for the encouragement and promotion of such manufactories as will tend to render the United States, independent on foreign nations for military, and other essential supplies." It is an exhaustive document, showing the results of research on the physical economy of the country which Hamilton, aided by his Treasury associate Tench Coxe, had carried out over the previous two years, as well as the fruits of Hamilton's studies of economic theory over the previous decade. Because the *Report* devotes considerable space to dealing with economic theory, and was never explicitly voted upon, it has often been considered to have subsidiary importance, as compared to the papers on funding the debt and the national banking system, which were enacted into law.

In its totality, the *Report on Manufactures* spells out how Hamilton saw the Federal government's role in moving to industrialize and upgrade the United States into a fully sovereign, thriving republic which could resist threats from imperial powers, provide for the necessities of a growing population, and develop into a technological powerhouse to equal or surpass any other nation on Earth. It represents a vision of the future *diametrically opposite* to that of both the Southern plantation oligarchy, and the strictly mercantile financial oligarchy which had opposed his financial system. Hamilton's argumentation makes clear why he opposed slavery and fought for Federal government supremacy on those matters essential to maintaining the Union. It also defines the subsuming purpose of his financial system. As we will elaborate later, this document had the most far-reaching international impact of any of his work.

While there is no substitute for reading (and re-reading) the *Report on Manufactures* itself, its importance dictates a thorough summary here. I will begin with reviewing Hamilton's theoretical discussion; the following chapter will deal with his specific recommendations and actions to implement his plan.

Economic Theory

From the outset of the *Report*, Hamilton turns to refuting the "respectable patrons of opinion, unfriendly to the encouragement of manufactures." He clearly has Adam Smith[2] in mind but does not jump right in to deal with Smith's "invisible hand" argument. Rather, Hamilton first utilizes the arguments which Smith himself used to take on the notions of the Physiocrats, who argued that "Agriculture is, not only, the most productive, but the only productive, species of industry."

The Physiocrats, who were based in France, insisted that only the cultivation of land produces a profit; riches are what Nature provided you to dig up out of the ground. Thus, they deny the role of human creativity in creating wealth, and insist that manufacturing adds nothing of additional value to the economy. This view is reflected in their fetishism about a whole class of natural resources such as gold, silver, and other ores. Their outlook was the logical concomitant of a feudalistic style of life, where labor (serfdom) was indeed bound to the land, and where the workers of the land were treated as just another adjunct to the physical property owned by the feudal lord. The coherence of the feudalistic view with the outlook of the Southern slavocracy cannot be missed.

Smith attacked the Physiocratic theory, arguing that labor in manufacturing does add to the annual product of a country, and that its productivity can be increased by such measures as increasing the division of

---

[2] While a discussion of the *Report on Manufactures* demands discussion of Adam Smith's opposition to Americans turning to manufactures, I have postponed a fuller treatment of Smith's economic outlook to Chapter 7.

labor, and by workers learning new skills. But he says that this process only occurs by taking resources away from agriculture. It requires "parsimony" (extreme frugality) or taking savings from agriculture to fund manufactures. In other words, a zero-sum game.

Smith's outlook contrasts fundamentally with that of Hamilton's American System and exemplifies what might be described as the difference between a credit system and a money system of economy. In a credit system, money is advanced on the basis that the investment will produce an improvement in the economy of the future. It is known that there will likely be no immediate "return on investment," but that there could be a long-term gain in productivity and production. In a money system such as Smith is advocating, the investor has to accumulate the means to launch an investment from his existing resources. Such a money system leads to an obsession with accumulating hard currencies and cutting expenses, but no understanding of how to produce economic growth.[3]

After challenging the Physiocratic outlook, Hamilton takes on Smith himself. Smith's theory deals with the relative value and mechanics of exchange (trade), including that between the agricultural and

---

[3] For a lively description of the difference between a credit system and one based on hard money, see Michael Kirsch, "The Credit System vs. Speculation: Nicholas Biddle and the 2nd Bank of the United States," *Executive Intelligence Review*, July 20, 2012.

manufacturing sectors of a nation, as well as between nations. One key fallacy in this approach is that trade *per se* does not *create* wealth. Trade also generally represents the attempt by the stronger nation to get what it needs at the lowest possible price, and to sell what it has at the highest possible, in the interest of short-term profit and long-term control.

Hamilton ran into this mindset in the young United States as well, especially within the mercantile class in the North, many members of which were perfectly happy to make huge profits on foreign trade, rather than carry out the long-term investment in the manufacturing and infrastructural base of their own country which Hamilton knew was necessary to increase the productivity and prosperity of the economy.

The Treasury Secretary then turns to his own argument: "that manufacturing establishments not only occasion a positive augmentation of the Produce and Revenue of the Society, but that they contribute essentially to rendering them *greater* than they could possibly be, without such establishments" [emphasis added]. How this occurs he then elaborates in seven conceptually rich propositions, which are worthy of our close scrutiny.

The integrated Saugus ironworks in Massachusetts, established in the 17th century, was an early challenger to English dominance of manufacturing, and helped provoke English countermeasures to prohibit the colonies from producing iron products. Hamilton was determined to gain self-sufficiency in this vital area of the economy. A national park recreates the facility today. (stock. adobe.com)

The Benefits of Manufacturing

Hamilton's listing of the benefits of manufacturing for the nation proceeds as follows:

1. Hamilton first notes manufacturing's importance in promoting the *division of labor*, which will improve workers' particular skills through specialization, and thus increased efficiency. He singles out the crucial role of the "fabrication of Machines," what would be called today the machine–tool industry, in extending

the "productive powers of labour,"[4] and thus the total product or revenue of the country.

2. Point two is *an extension of the use of Machinery*," which represents the addition of "artificial" labor to what man can do with his own hands. The productivity benefits of such an application should best be achieved in the home country, he argues, rather than depending upon more mechanized production elsewhere (as in the cotton industry in England). Later on, he refers specifically to recent improvements in machinery, achieved by "substituting the Agency of fire and water" for manual labor.

3. Point three is *the additional employment of classes of the community*," by which Hamilton means the recruitment of persons otherwise idle for one reason or another, including women and children. While the use of child labor is clearly distasteful to us today, in the era where it was ubiquitous on the farm, it did not appear so shocking.

4. Point four is *the promoting of emigration from foreign countries.*" Hamilton here is anticipating what was already underway as a major migration from Europe to the United States. Unstated

---

[4] The concept of the "productive powers of labor" is central to the American System of political economy throughout its history, one of the most notable expositions being Abraham Lincoln's campaign stump speech on Discoveries and Inventions. See the text here.

in the *Report*, but explicit in Hamilton's correspondence on the Society for Useful Manufactures (SUM), is his commitment to recruiting skilled labor from Europe to augment progress in manufacturing—a direct challenge to Great Britain's explicit policy of prohibiting "technology transfer" to other countries, especially the American colonies. In 1774, Britain banned the emigration of mechanics to its colonies, and the laws got even more punitive after the American colonies won their independence, up until at least 1824. Hamilton (and his co-thinkers such as Benjamin Franklin) had no intention of complying.[5]

Hamilton then turns to the crucial subjective side of his pro-manufacturing policy. Points five and six—*"furnishing greater scope for the diversity of talents and dispositions,"* and *"affording a more ample and various field for enterprise"*—deal with the impact of his policy on the human mind. They represent Hamilton's acknowledgement that it is the strong, active powers of the inventive intellect upon which the advancement of manufacturing, and thus the nation's prosperity, depend. Hamilton notes that it is already said that "there is, in the genius of the people of this country, a peculiar aptitude for mechanic improvements," and that

---

[5] See Peter Andreas, *Smuggler Nation: How Illicit Trade Made America*, Oxford University Press, 2013.

this should be an additional inducement to promoting manufactures.

Hamilton then makes one of his characteristic arguments on the question of exertion, or energy, in government and economy. He writes: *"To cherish and stimulate the activity of the human mind, by multiplying the objects of enterprise, is not among the least considerable of the expedients, by which the wealth of a nation may be promoted."*

This encomium to the spirit of enterprise should not be seen narrowly as a nod to the profit motive— as many "pro-Hamilton" thinkers do today–but as a statement about the role of the spirit of invention, of creative thought, and of a state of mind conducive to shaping the world around one. Hamilton believed in determining world events, with ideas and actions, not just responding to them, and energy of mind was thus a crucial quality to foster, as much as energy in government.[6]

This point is of critical importance to understanding his theory of political economy. Hamilton was no materialist. He believed that the human mind was the source of inventiveness and thus productivity, a view which led to his particular concept of credit, and

---

[6] This viewpoint is reflected in one of Hamilton's mottos, which comes from the Greek statesman Demosthenes [4th Century BC]: "As a general marches at the head of troops, so ought wise politicians, if I dare use the expression, to march at the head of affairs; insomuch that they ought not to await the event, to know what measures to take, but the measures which they have taken ought to produce the event."

of the government's need to foster the arts, sciences, and technology. This outlook was elaborated even more explicitly by Hamilton's successors, such as the German-American economist Friedrich List and Abraham Lincoln's chief economic advisor Henry C. Carey. List wrote of a "capital of mind," in addition to the "capital of nature" and "capital of productive matter,"[7] as the essential components of a productive economy. Attention to the "capital of mind" is critical to determining a nation's labor, education, and cultural policy—which are more infinitely more critical to determining a nation's wealth than its natural resources.

Hamilton's seventh and final listed benefit of manufacturing, which he calls the most important, is that it creates a steady demand for agriculture products. Thus "it is a principal mean, by which the establishment of manufactures contributes to an augmentation of the produce or revenue of a country, and has an immediate and direct relation to the prosperity of Agriculture." Agriculture, then the greatest segment of the economy, needs a solid and growing domestic market, he argues, and the dependence upon foreign buyers is insecure indeed. Therefore, promoting manufacturing is the best thing you can do for agriculture, as well as for the country as a whole.

---

[7] See Friedrich List, *Outlines of American Political Economy in Twelve Letters to Charles J. Ingersoll*, a new translation, Dr. Böttiger Verlag-GMBH, Wiesbaden, 1996, p. 59.

ANSWERING THE CRITICS

Before turning to his specific proposals for government promotion of manufacturing, Hamilton goes on to answer certain key criticisms of his proposal for an active manufacturing or industrial policy for the United States. These include:

1. Countering the idea that the U.S. can benefit from free trade. Hamilton argues correctly that a "system of perfect liberty to industry and commerce" doesn't exist, but rather one "regulated by an opposite spirit." Thus lack of manufactures and dependence on other nations will lead to an unstable market, impoverishment, and vulnerability.

2. Refuting the idea that establishing manufactures will retard western expansion. Hamilton argues that agriculture's interests would be best advanced by being accompanied by the growth of manufactures; he, like Lincoln later, wanted to see the country grow by establishing centers of civilization, not farming in the wilderness. But Hamilton asserts that the desire for land ownership is so strong that the progress of new settlements will not be retarded by manufacturing growth.

3. Overcoming the possible shortage of labor, both by use of machinery and immigration. Hamilton takes particular note of "a very pregnant and

instructive fact"; "the vast extension given by late improvements to the employment of Machines, which substituting the Agency of fire and water, had prodigiously lessened the necessity of manual labour."

4. Dealing with the high cost of labor in America relative to Europe: This can be done by mechanization and improved infrastructure in transportation. Hamilton believes the entrepreneur in the United States can afford to pay higher wages than in Europe, because, although wages in America are higher than in Europe, other costs like transportation are less.

5. Overcoming the lack of capital: This is answered with the establishment of the National Bank, made possible by the funding of the debt, which has become a "species of Capital." Hamilton goes on to say: "by serving as a new power in the operations of industry, it [the Bank— ed.] has within certain bounds a tendency to increase the real wealth of a Community, in like manner as money borrowed by a thrifty farmer, to be laid out in the improvement of his farm, may, in the end, add to his Stock of real riches."

6. Countering the idea that promoting domestic manufactures will create monopolies that fleece the people. Hamilton argues that even if prices do go up initially due to protection of domestic industry, "it is universally true, that the contrary is the ultimate effect with every successful

manufacture. When a domestic manufacture has attained to perfection, and has engaged in the prosecution of it a competent number of Persons, it invariably becomes cheaper."

Hamilton concludes this section thus:

The objections which are commonly made to the expediency of encouraging, and to the probability of succeeding in, manufacturing pursuits, in the United States, having now been discussed, the Considerations which have appeared in the Course of the discussion, recommending that species of industry to the patronage of the Government, will be materially strengthened by a few general and some particular topics, which have been naturally reserved for subsequent Notice.

The Hamilton statue in New York City's Central Park. The statue by Carl Conrads was commissioned by Hamilton's son John, and dedicated in 1880. (courtesy of Nancy Spannaus)

CHAPTER 3

What the *Report on Manufactures* Proposes

And there seems to be no room for a doubt that whatever concerns the general Interests of Learning, *of* Agriculture, *of* Manufactures, *and of* Commerce *are within the sphere of the national Councils as far* as regards an application of Money. *[emph. in original]*

–Report on Manufactures

IN THE CONCLUSION to his report, Hamilton presents both general and very concrete arguments and proposals for the U.S. government's promotion of manufacturing. This section includes the results of the nation's first industrial survey which Hamilton had assembled, as well as his general conclusions. He starts with three general assertions.

Hamilton's first point is that "there seems to be a moral certainty, that the trade of a country which is both manufacturing and Agricultural will be more lucrative and prosperous than that of a Country, which is mere Agricultural."

Secondly, he argues:

> Not only wealth, but the independence and security of a Country, appear to be materially connected with the prosperity of manufactures. Every nation, with a view to those great objects, ought to endeavor to possess within itself all the essentials of national supply. These comprise the means of *Subsistence, habitation, clothing, and defence* [emphasis in the original].

> The possession of these is necessary to the perfection of the body politic; to the safety as well as to the welfare of the society; the want of either is the want of an important Organ of political life and Motion; and in the various crises which await a state, it must severely feel the effects of any such deficiency.

Hamilton's third and extremely critical point is that encouraging manufacturing is in the interests of *all* parts of the Union–North, South, East, and West. Hamilton had been making this argument from the time of his pamphlets in 1774-75, when he took on the British opponents of the growing Revolutionary movement, who were proposing that the interests of the merchants and city dwellers leading the boycotts of Britain were contrary to the interests of the farmers. That Tory argument had subsequently been taken up by the Jeffersonian party, and Hamilton never ceased in his efforts to prove its falsehood.

After noting that the experience of recent years had shown that "the *aggregate* prosperity of manufactures, and the *aggregate* prosperity of Agriculture are intimately connected," he argues that the opposite assertion is "unfriendly to the steady pursuit of one great common cause, and to the perfect harmony of all the parts." And in conclusion,

> It is a truth as important as it is agreeable, and one to which it is not easy to imagine exceptions, that *everything tending to establish substantial and permanent order in the affairs of a Country, to increase the total mass of industry and opulence, is ultimately beneficial to every part of it.* On the Credit of this great truth, an acquiescence may be safely be accorded, from every quarter, to all institutions & arrangements which promise a confirmation of public order, and an augmentation of National Resource. [emphasis added]

Hamilton's final general point addresses the complaint that foreign investors had flocked to purchase U.S. government debt, including investing in the Bank of the United States (BUS). While foreign shareholders did not have a vote in the Bank, fears of foreign influence were easy to excite. Hamilton argues that if the U.S. provides investment opportunities in manufacturing which attract foreign money, the country will be the gainer. But the opportunities offered for such investments should include "solid and permanent improvements" to the nation, such as opening canals and the like, which would benefit all sections of the economy.

Specific Options

Eleven specific measures the Federal government might take for promotion of manufacturing are outlined by Hamilton, one by one. These include "protecting duties," prohibition of "rival articles," prohibition of certain exports, pecuniary bounties[1] ("one of the most efficacious means of encouraging manufactures, and ... in some views, the best"), premiums, and the exemptions of the materials of manufacturers from duties.

The list begins with protecting duties, or tariffs, a measure which had already been put into effect by the new government. Tariffs are particularly important

---

[1] See glossary.

because they bring in revenue, Hamilton notes, as well as the fact that they aid manufactures when the duties are not applied to raw materials by allowing "National Manufacturers to undersell all their foreign Competitors."

Hamilton pays an extraordinary amount of attention to bounties, which, he argues, do not increase the direct cost of the item to the consumer. In addition, they are "more positive and direct"; don't have a tendency to create scarcity; and are the "only proper expedient" for encouraging new objects of agriculture and manufacture. He proposes combining tariffs on certain imports with bounties to promote their domestic manufacture. After all, Hamilton says, "the duty upon the importation of an article can no otherwise aid the domestic production of it."

(This point is quite relevant to the argument about the role of tariffs today: Tariffs are an adjunct, not a substitute, for a credit policy to expand industrial growth.)

To those who complain about spending government money to advance manufactures, Hamilton argues: "It is the Interest of the society in each case, to submit to the temporary expense, which is more than compensated, by an increase of industry and Wealth, by an augmentation of resources and independence, & by the circumstances of eventual cheapness, which has been noticed in another place." And as to the constitutionality of such measures? Hamilton argues for a broad construction on spending for the "general Welfare," concluding:

> It is therefore of necessity left to the discretion of the National Legislature, to pronounce, upon the objects, which concern the general Welfare, and for which under that description, an appropriation of money is requisite and proper. And there seems to be no room for a doubt that whatever concerns the general Interests of *Learning*, of *Agriculture*, of *Manufactures*, and of *Commerce* are within the sphere of the national Councils *as far as regards an application of Money.*

> The only qualification of the generality of the Phrase in question, which seems to be admissible, is this—That the object to which an appropriation of money is to be made be *General* and not *local;* its operation extending in fact, or by possibility, throughout the Union, and not being confined to a particular spot. [emphasis in original]

Before turning to his proposals for developing and protecting specific industries, Hamilton adds two crucial policy proposals. The first is "the encouragement of new inventions and discoveries," in which he calls for extending measures which had been passed in An Act to promote the progress of Arts (April 10, 1790), to introducers of technological improvements. In his concluding section, he elaborates on this theme in a discussion of how an anticipated surplus in the revenue from duties may be used:

First. To constitute a fund for paying the bounties which shall have been decreed.

Secondly. To constitute a fund for the operations of a Board to be established, for promoting Arts, Agriculture, Manufactures and Commerce.

The model which Hamilton cites for constituting such a Board is the Pennsylvania Society for Promotion of Manufactures and Useful Arts, a group organized contemporaneously with the Constitutional Convention by Tench Coxe, Robert Morris, Gouverneur Morris, and Mathew Carey, at the home of Benjamin Franklin.[2]

Hamilton also proposes "the facilitating of the transportation of commodities" through assisting the improvement of public roads and opening canals. He urges local governments to take up this effort, but puts forward the idea of a "comprehensive plan" by the national Government, noting that "this is one of those improvements, which could be prosecuted with more

---

[2] For elaboration on this society, see Anton Chaitkin, "Key Policy Paper Uncovered: How Benjamin Franklin Organized Our Economic Independence," *EIR*, Oct. 21, 2011. Coxe's address can be found at the Evans Early American Imprint Collection. You can click here.

efficacy by the whole than by any part or parts of the Union. There are cases in which the general interest will be in danger to be sacrificed to the collision of some supposed local interests. Jealousies are as apt to exist as they are apt to be erroneous."

SECTOR BY SECTOR

Hamilton devotes the rest of his report to going sector by sector through the economy, evaluating what should be done to promote each in light of five criteria:

1. the capacity of the United States to supply the raw material;
2. the degree to which the industry can replace manual labor with machinery;
3. the ease of executing the measure;
4. the extensiveness of the use of the article; and
5. the importance of the article to priorities such as national defense.

In each case, he evaluates the state of the industry and what measures he would recommend.

He begins with iron, which he considers entitled to "preeminent rank" because of its importance to national defense. He includes steel with iron. In this case he not only proposes tariffs but direct government involvement in the manufacture—a measure he says, "as a general rule," should be avoided, but not in this case.

The following industries are subsequently discussed: copper; lead; fossil coal; wood; skins; grain (this item includes distilled spirits, the area of domestic taxation which ultimately caused the biggest uproar in the country); flax and hemp; cotton (He proposes a repeal of the duty on imports, and bounties for home manufacture); wool; silk; glass; gun powder; paper; printed books; and refined sugars and chocolate. For some items he recommends bounties, for others premiums, some higher duties and some lower, or their elimination altogether. There is no "one size fits all" mindset here, but a careful analysis of what the country produces, what it needs, and how best to encourage what the nation needs.

The site of Hamilton's Society for Useful Manufactures at Great Falls. These falls provided a powerful source of hydropower for the complex Hamilton envisioned. The subsequent hydropower electric plant can be seen on the left. (photo courtesy of Leonard A. Zax)

THE SOCIETY FOR USEFUL MANUFACTURES

While he was preparing the *Report on Manufactures*[3], Hamilton took on the task of setting up a "pilot project," so to speak, for what he believed could be accomplished. The name of that project was the Society for Establishing Useful Manufactures (known as SUM), and its vision was nothing less than to establish a large, model manufacturing hub, run by hydropower, to compete successfully in areas as diverse as cotton goods, paper, shoes, and iron wire with the British imports which continued to flood the country. In addition, the SUM would be empowered to establish canals and raceways[4], and preside over the creation of the world's first planned industrial city, Paterson, New Jersey.

When the location was chosen, the Passaic Falls comprised the most powerful waterfall within the boundaries of the United States, and was thus a wonderful source of power for industry. The hydroelectric power plant at the Falls, built in 1914, still provides enough energy to light one-third of the city of Paterson (depending upon water conditions).

---

[3] Hamilton had sent out requests for information on the state of the country's manufactures to his contacts throughout the country. He was also aided by his assistant Secretary, Tench Coxe, who took over from Duer in the spring of 1790, and wrote a draft of the report which Hamilton substantially worked over.

[4] Raceways are channels made by diverting streams, generally to power mills.

Hamilton himself wrote the prospectus[5] for the Society, which was published in August of 1791. It began:

> The establishment of Manufactures in the United States when maturely considered will be <found> to be of the highest importance to their prosperity. It <is> an almost self-evident proposition that that com<muni>ty which can most completely supply its own w<ants> is in a state of the highest political perfection. <And> both theory and experience conspire to prove that a nation (unless from a very peculiar coincidence of circumstances) cannot possess much active wealth but as the result of extensive manufactures.

> While also it is manifest that the interest of the community is deeply concerned in the progress of this species of Industry, there is <as> little room to doubt that the interest of individuals may equally be promoted by the pursuit of it. What <is> there to hinder the profitable prosecution of manufact<ures> in this Country, when it is notorious, that, independent of impositions for the benefit of the

---

[5] The full prospectus can be found here. It is available from Founders Online, the site run by the National Archives.

revenue and for the encouragement of domestic enterprise—the natural commercial charges of the greater part of th<ose> which are brought from Europe amount to from fiftee<n to> thirty per Cent—and when it is equally notorious that provisions and various kinds of raw materials are ev<en> cheaper here than in the Country from which our principal supplies come?

To Hamilton, it was absolutely clear that the United States would never have true independence without producing its own essential goods. That point had been hammered home during the War, when the lack of military supplies crippled the Army. Now, to preserve what had been won, the need was also urgent. "America, to be free of British influence, must be industrially free," Hamilton said. If the SUM was successful, it would spur his plans for a national manufacturing policy.

Hamilton's prospectus was widely publicized, as well as circulated among potential investors. He was aiming at, and succeeded in, getting public support from the state of New Jersey, whose governor was William Paterson. The state agreed to charter the SUM as a corporation with the right to hold property, improve rivers, build canals, and raise funds through a lottery ($100,000 a year over five years was authorized). It even had the power to exercise eminent domain. In addition, the SUM would be exempt from local taxes for 10 years. The legislature granted the charter on Nov. 22, 1791, less than two weeks before the *Report on Manufactures* was issued.

As in the case of the Bank of the United States, Hamilton sought to link the public and private interests in this project. Stock in this quasi-public corporation, which was authorized up to $1 million, could be purchased with government bonds or stock from the Bank of the United States.

In the prospectus, Hamilton laid out how his design of the SUM would overcome the normal objections to manufacturing—specifically, the high price of labor and the lack of capital. He addressed those problems with arguments identical to those in the *Report on Manufactures*. The first problem would be addressed by an increase in the use of machinery; the second by the implementation of his financial system. He wrote:

> The last objection disappears in the eye of those who are aware how much may be done by a proper application of the public Debt. Here is the resource which has been hitherto wanted. And while a direction of it to this object may be made a mean of public prosperity and an instrument of profit to adventurers in the enterprise, it, at the same time, affords a prospect of an enhancement of the value of the debt; by giving it a new and additional employment and utility.

Hamilton was determined to use the Revolutionary War debt to invest in the nation's future, creating a source of credit that would spark an upward spiral of wealth in the nation as a whole. He also put a major effort into recruiting skilled labor from Europe, which he intended to use to train American workmen in the necessary skills.

As a review of the prospectus makes clear, Hamilton expected the SUM to lose money in the short term. But things turned out worse than he thought when greedy investors on the board of directors, starting with its president Duer, used the funds raised for the SUM to feed the speculative frenzy which they had instigated in New York City. This gave the enemies of Hamilton's perspective a useful weapon against him.

But contrary to the assertions of many, the SUM did not fail. As Leonard A. Zax, the president of the Hamilton Partnership for Paterson, testified to the Senate Subcommittee on National Parks in 2007, "by 1816, Paterson was already a national leader in many of the goods Hamilton had listed in the great state paper he had submitted to Congress, the *Report on Manufactures.* Just as Hamilton urged, Paterson avoided excessive dependence on any one industry and became an extraordinary center of invention and a major producer of a wide variety of goods."[6]

In his promotion of the creation of the Paterson Great Falls National Historical Park, Zax has also emphasized

---

[6] The testimony was given on behalf of the New Jersey Community Development Corporation on Sept. 27, 2007.

its role as a representation of Hamilton's vision for American industry and economic independence. It was a model of technological and engineering innovation, and, as economic historian Richard Sylla has noted,[7] was intended to, and did, serve as an "incubator" of entrepreneurial manufacturing startups.

Paterson was also a living example of Hamilton's alternative to Jefferson's rural (and slave-based) economy. It has attracted and nourished a diverse population throughout its history.

Utilizing Pierre L'Enfant's groundbreaking plan[8] of raceways to capture water from a major river for powering industry, the SUM opened its first mill in 1794. It closed in 1796, but by 1800, operations were underway again. As the biggest manufacturing complex in the nation, Paterson played a major role in provisioning the nation in the War of 1812. Eventually, its roster of industries included cotton, candles, paper, silk, the Colt revolver, and the first steam locomotive made entirely of American-made parts. By 1854, it was the largest producer of locomotives in the nation. By the late 19th Century, Paterson was known as Silk City.

---

[7] Sylla made his comments in a letter to Interior Secretary Gayle Norton in support of designating Great Falls a national park.

[8] The American Society of Civil Engineers and the American Society of Mechanical Engineers produced an illustrated pamphlet on the SUM entitled The Great Falls Raceway and Power System in 1977. It is online here.

The SUM continued in existence until 1945, when the City of Paterson bought all its stock. The city still owns the land and the hydroelectric plant.

SUCCESS

Ultimately, of course, Hamilton's ideas for developing a manufacturing powerhouse of a nation, through an active role of the Federal government in providing credit for economic growth, also found realization. His ideas were taken up by leading individuals in the Democratic-Republican Party (such as Mathew Carey), and became the basis for the "American System" nation-building policies of the Administrations of John Quincy Adams and Abraham Lincoln, and eventually, Franklin D. Roosevelt.

Hamilton himself had referenced a unique American System in *Federalist* no. 11: "Let Americans disdain to be the instruments of European greatness! Let the thirteen States, bound together in a strict and indissoluble Union, concur in erecting one great *American system*, superior to the control of all transatlantic force or influence, and able to dictate the terms of the connection between the old and the new world!" [emphasis added].

Under his successors, this American System came to be defined as a three-point program comprising the National Bank (a national credit system), a system of protection (tariffs, support for labor and crucial industry), and internal improvements (what today we call infrastructure).

Contrary to the myth that fiscal-conservative and small-government policies built the United States, it was during the periods of time when Hamilton's policies of national banking and promotion of manufacturing prevailed, that the United States flourished.[9] I devote the next chapter to presenting that case.

---

[9] Academics have gone to great lengths to suppress this truth. For example, a doctoral thesis by Frank Bourgin, submitted to the University of Chicago in 1945, was rejected because it challenged this myth. See *The Great Challenge, The Myth of Laissez-Faire in the Early Republic*, Frank Bourgin, 1989, Braziller press.

The Second Bank of the United States, located in Philadelphia, Pa.
(stock.adobe.com)

CHAPTER 4

Hamilton's ideas of political economy formed the basis for America's periods of prosperity.

Public Credit ... is among the principal engines of useful enterprise and internal improvement. As a substitute for capital, it is little less useful than gold or silver, in agriculture, in commerce, in the manufacturing and mechanic arts....

—Report on the Plan for Further
Support of Public Credit

THERE HAVE BEEN four periods in United States' history in which Hamilton's American System principles were successfully implemented, although not often explicitly identified with his name. The continuity proceeds from his collaborators such as Philadelphia publisher Mathew Carey (1760-1839). As the editor of the *American Museum* magazine (1788-1792), and later as a participant in many Pennsylvania societies for the promotion of manufacturing, Carey fought successfully to win over a faction of Jefferson's Democratic-Republican Party to Hamilton's economic perspective. Carey's seminal document for this purpose was the 1814 *Olive Branch*, a biting attack on the errors of both the Federalists and the Democratic-Republicans. In the case of the Democratic-Republicans, he identified their flaw as abandoning Hamilton's policy of the National Bank and industrial development, an error for which the nation paid dearly during the War of 1812.

Carey's circle of collaborators included Nicholas Biddle (1786-1844), president of the Second Bank of the United States during John Quincy Adams' presidency (1825-1829); Friedrich List, a German economist who spent from 1825 to 1832 in Pennsylvania learning from the Carey circles and promoting their policies; a number of newspaper editors; and ultimately his son Henry C. Carey, who became the chief economic advisor to President Abraham Lincoln.

Through Carey and Lincoln, Hamilton's American System ideas became institutionalized within the Republican Party, and were carried forward even after Carey's death in 1879. But after the murder of President McKinley (who was assassinated September 1901), Hamilton's economic policies were nominally coopted by a pro-imperialist section of the party, epitomized by Boston Brahmins like Henry Cabot Lodge, and associated with both high finance and anti-labor policies. Thus, when Franklin Roosevelt, who boasted of his descent from Hamilton collaborator Isaac Roosevelt,[1] proceeded to implement Hamiltonian policies to deal with the national bankruptcy brought on by the speculators who caused the Great Depression, he chose to identify his policies with Hamilton's opponent Thomas Jefferson. Jefferson was then built up as the exemplar of the fighter for the "common man," despite the fact that his economic policies by and large represented the very opposite.

But it was Hamilton's legacy of Federal government supervision of banking, protection of the working man and domestic industry, and launching internal improvements which FDR actually carried out through his Presidential terms. And it was FDR's economic approach to which President John F. Kennedy turned, and sought to revive during his very brief Presidency.

In the rest of this chapter and the next two, I present the evidence that it was during the periods that the national leadership of the United States worked from Hamiltonian principles that the nation became a great industrial and economic power. In all of those periods, the Federal government used government-backed credit to foster economic growth, defend

---

[1] A full discussion of FDR's pride in his connection to his great-great-grandfather Isaac Roosevelt, who collaborated with Hamilton in the New York State ratifying convention for the U.S. Constitution (1788) and the Bank of New York, can be found here. It is in the article "Then and Now: Why Roosevelt's Explosive 1933-1945 Recovery Worked," by Richard Freeman, *EIR*, April 26, 2002.

national sovereignty, and control speculators. Those periods are: 1) the Washington Administration; 2) the John Quincy Adams Administration; 3) the Lincoln Administration; and 4) the Administration of Franklin Delano Roosevelt.

THE WASHINGTON ADMINISTRATION

Key to the success of the Washington Administration was the creation of the First Bank of the United States (BUS), the brainchild of his Treasury Secretary Alexander Hamilton.[2] When Washington became President, the United States was drowning in its enormous Revolutionary War debt, which was owed to states, individuals, and foreign governments. Not even interest was being paid, and due to 1) the lack of an income stream to the national government, 2) the destruction from the war, and 3) the continued economic and physical onslaught by the British against the fledgling new government, the very survival of the nation was at risk. To save it, Hamilton reorganized the debt, had the Federal government assume the states' debts, and funded the management of the new debt instruments (government bonds)—the regular payment of interest–by new excise taxes and import duties.

---

[2] It should be acknowledged that Hamilton worked closely with other Revolutionary leaders, especially the "American Financier" Robert Morris, in developing his banking plan.

Congress created the Bank of the United States in 1791, and capitalized it at $10 million, a sum that was greater than that held by all the banks in the country at the time. And it was capitalized in one day! To summarize: Hamilton offered holders of the newly reorganized debt instruments the opportunity to invest in the bank. They could buy shares with one-quarter specie (gold, silver, coin, etc.) and three-quarters new government bonds. Shareholders would be paid a regular interest (six percent limit), all federally guaranteed. The interest on the newly minted government debt which the Bank held was paid to the Bank. The Bank was authorized to lend to the Federal government, but not to trade in government debt.

The Bank, established in Philadelphia, could issue currency notes up to the amount of its capital, $10 million, and that ability played a crucial role in finally permitting the funding of commerce and infrastructure (internal improvements) in the country. Those BUS notes became the new currency of the country, replacing the hundreds of foreign coins and/or private bank drafts that were otherwise circulating. The value of the currency was regulated by the Bank, and its investment in new productivity cemented its strong value. Also, the Bank of the United States was the sole depository of all government funds and federal taxes.

While many discussions of the BUS emphasize its role as a lender to the Federal government, its more substantive accomplishment was the stabilization of the currency, which aided all commercial transactions. Also often overlooked is its crucial accomplishment of turning debt into the basis for credit, a transformation which financially fixated economists still don't understand.[3]

The major source of funds used by the national government to pay interest on the government bonds was the revenue from the tariffs passed during the 1990s, as well as the domestic excise taxes which became such a political flashpoint in anti-Federal government areas. In addition, the Federal government received some revenue from the sale of Federal lands.

Credit from the Bank became the engine of economic growth of the country. Hamilton described the process thus in his final report to Congress in 1795:

> Public Credit ... is among the principal
> engines of useful enterprise and internal
> improvement. As a substitute for capital,
> it is little less useful than gold or silver,
> in agriculture, in commerce, in the
> manufacturing and mechanic arts.... It is
> a matter of daily experience in the most
> familiar pursuits. One man wishes to
> take up and cultivate a piece of land; he
> purchases upon credit, and, in time, pays
> the purchase money out of the produce of
> the soil improved by his labor. Another
> sets up in trade; in the credit founded

---

[3] For my earlier treatment of this breakthrough, see "A Matter of Principle: How Hamilton's Economics Created Our Constitution," *EIR*, December 10, 2010, accessible here.

upon a fair character, he seeks, and often
finds, the means of becoming, at length,
a wealthy merchant. A third commences
business as manufacturer or mechanic,
with skill, but without money. It is
by credit that he is enabled to procure
the tools, the materials, and even the
subsistence of which he stands in need,
until his industry has supplied him with
capital; and, even then, he derives, from
an established and increased credit, the
means of extending his undertakings.

Growth was steady, though not at the pace reached
under later such facilities, simply because the nation
was starting at "square one." Nevertheless, the results
were impressive.[4]

Production of useful materials expanded at a rapid
rate. Merchandise exports had quintupled by 1805,
with well over $100 million exported. Gross tonnage
moving across the oceans in American-built vessels
doubled. Imports had grown more rapidly.

From 1803 to 1807, an average of 80 patents per
year were issued for new inventions, a rate four times
greater than from 1790-1794. Twenty thousand miles
of post roads were built, a nascent manufacturing base
was begun, and dams and early canals were constructed.

---

[4] Many authors emphasize U.S. gains through the growth of
commerce; here I stress the growth of the productive base of
the U.S. domestic economy.

Factories began to replace small proprietorships.[5] The steam engine began to be applied not only to navigation, but also to production facilities. Congress issued a down payment on creating the National Road, which played a key role in Western expansion.

One critical accomplishment was the establishment of West Point[6] in 1802, the culmination of efforts by Hamilton, Washington, Knox, and Adams during the 1790s to get a corps of engineers established. Hamilton's letters show he was totally committed to getting an educated corps of "artificers" who would be available to build infrastructure—as the Army Corps of Engineers has done throughout its long history. But progress was slow. By 1811, when the BUS charter expired, the main issue holding back the continued expansion of the productive economy was a lack of an adequate network of transportation.

One important measure of the accelerating growth potential was the increase in population. From 1790 to 1805, the U.S. population grew from 3.9 million to 6.3 million, an annual growth rate of 3.2%. Immigrants were flooding into the country from Europe, not least because of ongoing wars, but also in search of economic opportunity. The phenomenal population growth rate

---

[5] See Lawrence A. Peskin, *Manufacturing Revolution, The Intellectual Origins of Early American Industry*, Johns Hopkins University Press, 2003, chapter 8.

[6] See Pam Lowry, "How the Army Corps of Engineers Helped to Build the American Nation," available at https://american systemnow.com.

had, of course, been anticipated and encouraged by Hamilton. It reflected the idea, later elaborated by American System economists such as Henry Carey, that population is a primary source of wealth for an economy, and must be nourished as such.

The BUS turned a profit, despite the fact that its function had been bastardized by Jefferson's Treasury Secretary Albert Gallatin, as primarily a source for paying off the national debt. It was chartered for 20 years, but vigorous opposition from landed gentry and their financier allies prevented the charter from being renewed, thus leaving the nation at the mercy of private financiers as it entered the War of 1812.

Among the major projects launched under the J.Q. Adams Administration, were the railroads, which transformed economic life. Steam engines like the one shown in this engraving began to criss-cross the country, starting in the East.

THE JOHN QUINCY ADAMS ADMINISTRATION

John Quincy Adams came into office in 1825 as a supporter of the American System movement which had been launched by the Careyites; Henry Clay had been leading the fight as a Congressmen since the end of the War of 1812. Adams aspired to utilize the period of relative peace during his Administration to carry out grand projects of public improvement that would live through the ages. While he didn't achieve all he wished, his one term in office saw a dramatic leap up in the productive powers of the nation.[7]

Key to Adams' successes was the Second Bank of the United States which was chartered by Congress in 1816. It was capitalized in the same manner as the First Bank, with the investment of Treasuries into the Bank in exchange for shares. Since the Bank was created in a period where the economy was larger, investment in the Second Bank from private capital grew more rapidly than it did under the First Bank. Just like its predecessor, the Second Bank was chartered to carry out the expansion of the economy, not to bail out the government.

The original capital of the Bank was $35 million, of which $7 million was supplied by the government. This was a large amount, as the total amount of money

---

[7] See "America's Stunning Growth under the Second National Bank," by Anton Chaitkin, at https://americansytemnow.com. You can click here.

in circulation was $75 million, and annual revenue into the Federal government at that point was $25 million.

The Second Bank got off to a rocky start due to mismanagement, but when Nicholas Biddle became its President in 1823, the Bank made tremendous progress. Biddle came from the Pennsylvania circle of Benjamin Franklin and Mathew Carey, and had been head of the Pennsylvania Society for the Promotion of Internal Improvements. Biddle and Carey founded the Franklin Institute in Philadelphia to promote scientific research in aid of industrialization. Biddle had absorbed Hamiltonian principles as to how to create technological progress and build the nation. In a speech before the Pennsylvania State Legislature on January 3, 1811, dedicated to trying to get Congress to re-charter the BUS, Biddle blasted the idea that banks such as the BUS were tools of an oligarchy out to oppress the masses:

> To my mind no principle of national economy is clearer, than that the most natural way of protecting the poorer classes of a society is by a [national] bank: an institution ... which enables the farmer to reserve his crops for a better market, instead of sacrificing them for his immediate wants; and by loans, at a moderate rate of interest, reliev[ing] every class of society from the pressure of usury.

During the fight to defend the Second Bank from its critics in the 1830s, in a letter to John Quincy Adams, Biddle restated the Bank's positive role for the common man:

> In truth the banks are but the mere agents of [the] community. They have no funds not already lent out to the people, of whose property and industry they are the representatives. They are only other names for the farms, the commerce, the factories, and the internal improvements of the country....[8]

Under the guidance of Biddle, in tandem with President John Quincy Adams and Henry Clay as Speaker of the House, the economy rapidly expanded. Collaboration between the Congress and the Bank flourished, despite a tremendous pushback by speculators and opponents of industrial development.

As the *Niles Register* put it during that fight:

> The bank, because of the facilities which it affords in the exchanges, as well as on account of the uniformity in the currency which it establishes, is now

---

[8] Letter to John Quincy Adams on the Specie Circular, April 5, 1838. This was in response to President Jackson's executive order that payment for Federal lands had to be made in gold or silver, rather than currency.

a splendid pillar in the broad "American System;" for a large part–perhaps two-thirds of all its accommodations, in one way or another, are for the direct encouragement and extension of agriculture and the mechanic arts, the promotion of internal improvements, and erection of all sorts of buildings–dwellings and stores, and factories and workshops.... The power of this institution was once possessed by speculators–stock and money jobbers, monopolizing its means and playing into each other's hands.[9]

The Second Bank was directly involved in the development of canals, railroads, roads, the iron and coal industries, and state and local infrastructure projects. The overall standard of living of the nation grew as a result.

Some examples of the investments the Bank made in collaboration with either states or private capital included:

Railroads—The Bank helped fund (up to 50%) and create over 20 new rail lines across the nation. They included the Buffalo and Niagara Falls; the Philadelphia, Wilmington, and Baltimore; and many others.

---

[9] *Niles' Weekly Register,* Vol. XLIII, September. 22, 1832

On July 4, 1828 President Adams dug the first shovelful of dirt to begin construction of the Chesapeake & Ohio Canal. Shown here is an aqueduct over the Monocacy River, built as part of the canal between 1829 and 1833. (photo courtesy of Nancy Spannaus)

Canals—The Bank directly funded (again up to half the cost) eight canals, including the Brunswick in Georgia, the Illinois and Michigan, and the Morris Canal in New Jersey.

Coal—The Bank directly funded much of the new coal industry in Pennsylvania.

The Second Bank also financed turnpikes, roads, and bridges. Currency was controlled, the value of the dollar maintained, and credit was directed into infrastructure and industry. Biddle was also successful in his dealing with foreign exchange, and, according to leading banking historian Bray Hammond, he succeeded in shifting the balance of foreign exchange trade against the powerful British banking house, Barings Brothers. Clearly, British bankers were not happy.

Also unhappy were some major British-linked banking houses in the New York City financial establishment. As Hammond put it: The Second Bank was "a victim of the `money power,' which used Andrew Jackson, states' rights, and agrarian sentiment to destroy it." That "money power" wanted to move the financial center of the country to Wall Street. The Banks' "effective adversaries were not farmers but business men," Hammond asserts.[10]

The Second Bank's charter was renewed by Congress in 1832, but vetoed by President Andrew Jackson, who proceeded in 1833 to take U.S. government monies out of it and return to "hard money." The number of banks in the country skyrocketed, and, since there were no controls on what these banks had to keep for reserve requirements, pure speculation reigned. Such "deregulation" brought chaos of the sort we've seen in 1929 and 2008. Jackson's actions directly led to the Panic of 1837 and the downward spiral of the economy which lasted well into the 1840s.

TWENTY YEARS OF STAGNATION

In 1841, the Congress, under the leadership of Clay, passed new legislation chartering a Third Bank of the United States on the model of the first two. The bill passed both Houses, but was vetoed by President Tyler, who was beholden to the Southern slaveholders and

---

[10] Hammond, Bray, *Banks and Politics in America, from the Revolution to the Civil War*, Princeton University Press, Princeton, N.J., 1957.

northern Wall Street financiers. Tyler had become President as a result of the untimely death of Whig President William Henry Harrison.

The Whig Party, formed in opposition to President Jackson's contempt for the separation of powers and his destruction of the Bank of the United States, struggled to maintain a common program. To the extent it did, it could be summarized as the young Whig Abraham Lincoln did in announcing his campaign for Congress in 1832: "My politics are short and sweet, like the old woman's dance. I am in favor of a National bank. I am in favor of the internal improvement system and a high protective tariff. These are my sentiments and political principles."

The Whig Party never got to implement its positive program. The second President it elected, Zachary Taylor, died in office of an unknown ailment. From 1841 until the Presidency of Lincoln, the financial system was "deregulated." Over 7,000 different currencies were put into circulation, and thousands of banks of all shapes and sizes dotted the landscape, creating economic chaos, and a collapse of credit. Thanks to this disarray, and a number of pro-slavery Presidents, the expansion of infrastructure (especially transportation), industry, and urbanization into the Southern states which had been on the agenda of the Hamiltonians since the founding of the republic, never occurred.

The nation had to wait for the emergence of a new American System leader, Abraham Lincoln.

Abraham Lincoln, portrayed in an 1881 engraving.

CHAPTER 5

Abraham Lincoln, Hamiltonian

Let Americans disdain to be the instruments of European greatness! Let the thirteen States, bound together in a strict and indissoluble Union, concur in erecting one great American system, superior to the control of all transatlantic force or influence, and able to dictate the terms of the connection between the old and the new world!

–Alexander Hamilton, *Federalist* no. 11

JUST AS ALEXANDER Hamilton and George Washington were faced with creating a national political economy out of the chaos that followed the Revolutionary War, so Abraham Lincoln (1809-1865) faced the need to recreate national unity out of the violent strife of the Civil War. Not surprisingly, Lincoln turned to Hamilton's American System.

71

Candidate Abraham Lincoln, a protégé of Henry Clay, began as a Whig politician in Illinois, where he championed the building of infrastructure, especially railroads, to advance the state's economy. His Presidential campaign was run on the platform of the newly created Republican Party, and included internal improvements, a protective tariff, and a National Bank. Lincoln personally added the Transcontinental Railroad to the 1860 Republican platform. The policy of internal improvements, a tariff, and a National Bank had been dubbed the American System by Clay.

Lincoln shared two cardinal passions with American System founder Hamilton. The first was his commitment to fostering the productive powers of labor, which he saw as the crucial source of wealth and progress in the economy. He addressed this point directly in his 1860 campaign <u>speech</u> on Discoveries and Inventions, as well as expressing it in his abhorrence of slavery. The second was his commitment to the Constitutional Union as the bedrock for achieving the freedoms and prosperity the American population deserved.

Lincoln's approach to economic policy while in office also owes a lot to the man who became his chief economic advisor, Henry C. Carey (1793-1879). Carey's ideas represent a direct continuity from those of his father, Hamilton collaborator Mathew Carey, and also carried us forward into the period after Lincoln's death, when U.S. industrial progress stunned the world.

Carey's formulation of the American System deserves a close look.

HENRY CAREY, CHAMPION OF THE AMERICAN SYSTEM[1]

For 20 years before Abraham Lincoln became President, Henry C. Carey was working to establish himself as the leading political economist in the nation. In his 1840 book *Principles of Political Economy*, he took on British Malthusianism, arguing that a properly run economy will, through technological innovation and improvements in the productive powers of labor, embark on continuous progress, rather than reaching diminishing returns. The *Principles*, published in three volumes, became extremely popular, and the book was translated internationally.

Soon after, Carey took up his father's (and Hamilton's) cause of protecting industry, arguing that the British economic system (emphatically including free trade) was nothing more than a scheme for looting the rest of the world. Carey organized industrialists and others in Pennsylvania, his home base, in support of the productive tariff, and was an early leader of the Republican Party, promoting that plank of the Republican program.

In 1851, Carey embarked on a more polemical track with the publication of *The Harmony of Interest: Manufacturing, Agricultural, and Commercial*, in which he

---

[1] This section on Henry C. Carey is heavily based on the work of the late W. Allen Salisbury, author of the book *The Civil War and the American System: America's Battle with Britain, 1860-1876*.

argued for collaboration between labor, agriculture, and capital in a policy of protection and industrialization. He followed this up in 1853 with *The Slave Trade, Foreign and Domestic*, in which he argued that the slave system degrades the whole of society, free labor included; the book systematically documented the ups and downs of American industry depending upon the level of the protective tariff.

Carey played an active role in preparing the groundwork for Lincoln's victory in the 1860 election, taking specific aim at the "free trade" wing of the Republican Party and the radical abolitionists who were prepared to break up the Union on the issue of slavery. In a series of open letters to William Cullen Bryant, for example, Carey explicitly invoked Hamilton's perspective that "it was to the industrial element we were to look for the cement by which our people and our States were to be held together." If the nation were broken apart, it would lead to British domination of the continent and threaten republicanism itself.

As an alternative, Carey presented the American System, which he described so eloquently in the *Harmony of Interest:*

> Two systems are before the world; the one looks to increasing the proportion of persons and of capital engaged in trade and transportation, and therefore to diminishing the proportion engaged in producing commodities with which

to trade, with necessarily diminished return to the labour of all; while the other looks to increasing the proportion engaged in the work of production, and diminishing that engaged in trade and transportation, with increased return to all, giving the labourer good wages, and to the owner of capital good profits. One looks to increasing the quantity of raw materials to be exported, and diminishing the inducements to imports of men, thus impoverishing both farmer and planter by throwing on them the burden of freight; while the other looks to increasing the import of men, and diminishing the export of raw materials, thereby enriching both planter and farmer by relieving them from payment of freight. One looks to giving the products of millions of acres of land and of the labour of millions of men for the services of hundreds of thousands of distant men; the other to bringing the distant men to consume on the land the products of the land, exchanging day's labour for day's labour.

One looks to compelling the farmers and planters of the Union to continue their contributions for the support of the fleets and the armies, the paupers, the nobles, and the sovereigns of Europe; the other to enabling ourselves to apply the same means to the moral and intellectual improvement of the sovereigns of America. One looks to the continuance of that bastard freedom of trade which denies the principle of protection, yet doles it out as revenue duties; the other by extending the area of legitimate free trade by the establishment of perfect protection, followed by the annexation of individuals and communities, and ultimately by the abolition of customs houses. One looks to exporting men to occupy desert tracts, the sovereignty of which is obtained by aid of diplomacy or war; the other to increasing the value of an immense extent of vacant land by importing men by millions for their occupation. One looks to the centralization of wealth and power in a great commercial city that shall rival the great cities of modern times, which have been and are being supported by aid of contributions which have exhausted every nation subjected to them; the other to concentration, by aid of which a market shall be made upon the land for the products of the land, and the farmer and planter be enriched.

One looks to increasing the necessity of commerce; the other to increasing the power to maintain it. One looks to underworking the Hindoo, and sinking the rest of the world to his level; the other to raising the standard of man throughout the world to our level. One looks to pauperism, ignorance, depopulation, and barbarism; the other to increasing wealth, comfort, intelligence, combination of action, and civilization. One looks towards universal war; the other towards universal peace.

One is the English system; the other we may be proud to call the American system, for it is the only one ever devised the tendency of which was that of elevating while equalizing the condition of man throughout the world. [emphasis and paragraphing added][2]

---

[2] Click here, or see *Henry Carey - Excerpts from The Harmony of Interests: Agricultural, Manufacturing & Commercial* in American History, From Revolution to Reconstruction and beyond, www.let.rug.nl/USA/

LINCOLN'S MISSION

As President, Lincoln had no time to enact a new national bank; he was immediately confronted by the outbreak of the Civil War. By 1862 under the burden of war and rapidly diminishing finances, Lincoln and his collaborators found themselves toe-to-toe with the British-linked Wall Street financiers, who were demanding unacceptable measures in exchange for providing money to the Union. Under these conditions, Lincoln took the principle of National Banking and applied it to the crisis by creating a source of sovereign credit. He moved to centralize control over the nation's finances and direct credit to infrastructure and industry to win the Civil War and build the nation.

Congress passed three Legal Tender Acts in 1862 and 1863, which created a uniform circulating currency known as Greenbacks (the color of the ink on the back of the bills). In the Congressional debate over making the Greenbacks legal tender, Lincoln's allies in Congress explicitly cited the arguments of Alexander Hamilton in both the *Federalist* Papers and his opinion on the Constitutionality of the National Bank. Congressman Eldridge Spaulding of New York emphasized the importance of the greenback bill in allowing the government to provide for the common defense. He continued:

> Alexander Hamilton, in discussing these high powers of the Constitution

says: "These powers ought to exist,
WITHOUT LIMITATION; because
it is impossible to foresee or define
the extent and variety of national
exigencies and the correspondent extent
and variety of the means necessary to
satisfy them.... It must be admitted as a
necessary consequence, that there can
be NO LIMITATION of that authority
which is to provide for the defense and
protection of the community in any
matter essential to its efficacy; that is,
in any matter essential to the formation,
direction, or support of the NATIONAL
FORCES." (*Federalist* no. 23.[3])

Spaulding concluded: "I am unwilling that this
Government, with all its immense power and resources,
should be left in the hands of any class of men, bankers
or money-lenders.... Why, then, should it go into Wall
street, State street, Chestnut street, or any other street
begging for money? ...The powers of the Government
were given for the welfare of the nation. ... We need it
to prevent foreign intervention."

Circulation of the greenbacks, like the notes from
the First and Second Banks of the United States, allowed
both for payment of taxes and investment in needed
industrial and agricultural projects. Lincoln increased

---

[3] Click here.

the circulation of Greenbacks by 300% during his administration.

Not surprisingly, it was under Lincoln that Alexander Hamilton's picture first appeared on U.S. currency.[4] Both were confirmed nationalists, committed to using Federal power to "make a more perfect Union."

In 1863 and 1864 Congress passed the National Banking Acts based on the Hamiltonian model of the Banks of the United States. These acts created a national system, ending the chaotic reign of state and local banks running amok. Thousands of banks were re-chartered as part of the National Banking system. They were required to buy long-term Treasury bonds and deposit them with the Treasury as security, and the government then issued Greenbacks, backed by Treasury bills, to them to circulate. Interest on the Treasuries was funded with taxes and a tariff just like under George Washington and John Quincy Adams.

The legislation also created the Office of the Comptroller of the Currency to regulate this new national system. These acts by Lincoln remain at the core of today's U.S. banking system.

The results of this policy were impressive. Railroad development, much of it funded by Federal government land grants, drove much of the industrial economy. The U.S. erected a massive railway system, which

---

[4] Michael O'Malley, "The Ten-Dollar Founding Father," in *Historians on Hamilton, How a Blockbuster Musical is Restaging America's Past*, ed. Renee C. Romano & Claire Bond Potter, Rutgers U Press, New Jersey, 2018, pp. 129-130.

by 1865 extended to 45,000 miles. As the Lincoln policy continued after his death, railroad construction quadrupled to 167,000 miles by 1890, more than all the rail in Europe. Railroad development spurred expansion in all the related areas, i.e. bridge construction, tunnels, and raw materials mining. These included iron ore, coal, limestone, etc. Railroads were used for war-time troop transit and peacetime transportation. With the railroads came new cities and expanded agriculture, which was aided by the newly founded Department of Agriculture. Under Lincoln the Land Grant College and Homestead Acts fostered expanded education and population of the Midwest and Western states.

Lincoln began the Transcontinental Railroad, personally, in 1862. Even before the war, he had met with General Grenville Dodge to discuss the potential routes; he became expert in aspects of its development, including even gauges of the track. The Golden Spike in Utah which completed the rail line can be directly traced to Lincoln and his national banking policy. The northern spur of the railroad, the Union Pacific, was largely built by Union troops who migrated from rail construction during the war to the new lines opening up the West.

The United States also built the first modern telecommunication system during the war, the telegraphs. As the Transcontinental Railroad was building west, telegraph lines were being constructed alongside. When the system was connected at

Promontory Point, it was reported instantaneously by the new telegraph system.

Thanks to Lincoln, the Union was now bound together by transport and communications from coast to coast.

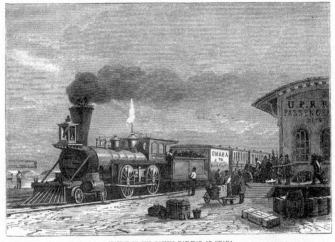

STATION OF THE PACIFIC RAILWAY AT OMAHA.

Uniting the nation coast to coast by rail was one of Lincoln's major achievements. Depicted here is a Pacific Railway train in Omaha, Nebraska, part of the transnational route.

A LASTING LEGACY

As a result of Lincoln's policies, the United States became an agro-industrial powerhouse, the envy of the world. Productivity expanded, as new inventions and new industrial output led to increasing rates of development and a massively growing economy. And despite concerted efforts by financiers to destroy Lincoln's system (they succeeded in cutting back the greenbacks dramatically with the Specie Resumption Act of 1879), the momentum caused by the Union policies in the war spurred further growth. That momentum was continued in no small measure by Henry Carey, who remained on the political scene until 1879.

The center for much of the innovation occurred in Philadelphia, the long-standing center of the Carey networks, both intellectual and industrial. Several entrepreneurs from that city had formed a partnership informally known as the "Philadelphia Interests," which controlled a unified set of large industrial companies. These included the Pennsylvania Railroad, the Baldwin locomotive company, the Denver & Rio Grande Railroad, the Pennsylvania Steel Company, the Kansas Pacific Railway, the Mexican National Railways, the Automatic Telegraph Company, and the owners of numerous other railroads, iron forges, machine builders, and coal mines. On the intellectual side, there was the scientist Alexander Dallas Bache and networks at the Franklin Institute and American Philosophical Society, the latter an institution which had included Hamilton in its ranks.

As demonstrated by historian Anton Chaitkin, this grouping set up and sponsored Thomas Alva Edison, the leading individual responsible for the breakthroughs in electricity that revolutionized American industry.[5]

---

[5] For discussion of the Philadelphia Interests and their sponsorship of Edison, see Anton Chaitkin, "Leibniz, Gauss Shaped

The growth spurred by Lincoln's and Carey's American System policies was dramatically show-cased in the 1876 Centennial Exposition in Philadelphia. The exposition, which drew more than nine million people over its six months' existence, put on display the astounding accomplishments of American industrial ingenuity and might. These included Alexander Graham Bell's telephone, Edison's phonograph, McCormick's reaper, Colt's repeating pistol, and most of all, Corliss's gigantic steam engine. The Baldwin locomotive company built a special engine just to go on display at the Exposition. In sum, the event showed the world that not only was the United States, still recovering from civil conflict, an equal to other nations in innovation and power; within two generations, it would be the most powerful nation on earth.

The Exposition drew dozens of international guests, including prominent representatives of Japan, Brazil, and Russia. The fruits of that visit, and associated international collaboration, soon became apparent in the adoption of American System-style policies throughout the world. I will take up this process, which created a mortal danger for the British imperial power still dominating the globe, in Chapter 9.

In the United States, however, the mantle was not taken up again until the Presidency of Franklin Roosevelt.

America's Science Successes," *Executive Intelligence Review*, Feb. 9, 1996.

President Franklin Delano Roosevelt signing Glass–Steagall during his 100 Days of emergency action against the Depression. (National Archives)

CHAPTER 6

Franklin Roosevelt Chose Hamilton

Public utility is more truly the object of public Banks, than private profit. And it is the business of Government, to constitute them on such principles, that while the latter will result, to a significant degree, to afford competent motives to engage in them, the former be not made subservient to it.

—Report on a National Bank

PRESIDENT FRANKLIN ROOSEVELT remains as the most vivid exemplar of the Hamiltonian approach to economy for people today. Renowned as the champion of Hamilton's opponent Thomas Jefferson, FDR in practice went back to the models of National Banking, and infrastructural and industrial development of the 19th Century. Not only FDR, but numbers of his advisors were versed in the American System tradition. Notable among them were Frances Perkins, Henry

Wallace, Harry Hopkins, Harold Ickes, and Sen. Robert Wagner.

FDR had a sense of personal connection to the Hamilton tradition which was evident at his home in Hyde Park, where a Gilbert Stuart portrait of his great-great-grandfather Isaac Roosevelt sat over the mantel of the fireplace. Dubbed "The Patriot," Isaac was a close collaborator of Hamilton at the New York State Ratifying Convention for the U.S. Constitution (1788), and later at the Bank of New York.

Presidential candidate FDR enunciated one of the key principles of Hamilton's thought—voluntarism—when he addressed the Democratic Party nominating convention in July 1932: "Our Republican leaders tell us economic laws—sacred, inviolable, unchangeable— cause panics which no one could prevent. But while they prate of economic laws, men and women are starving. We must lay hold of the fact that economic laws are not made by nature. They are made by human beings."[1]

This statement is an echo of Hamilton's arguments against the "natural course of things" put forward by Adam Smith, when Smith was arguing against the perspective of America embarking on industrialization. (See Chapter 7) Hamilton had determined that the welfare of the people demanded the development of manufactures, just as he had determined that an

---

[1] *The Essential Franklin Delano Roosevelt, FDR's Greatest Speeches, Fireside Chats, Messages, and Proclamations*, edited by John Gabriel Hunt, Gramercy Books, New York, 1995.

energetic Federal government gave him the tools to stop the Panic of 1792. FDR was following in his footsteps by declaring that a Constitutional government committed to the general welfare could challenge Wall Street's depredations against the population, and he proceeded to do so.

The well-educated FDR had learned his history well. As he laid out in his acceptance speech to the Democratic Convention in 1936, he knew that national sovereign governments such as Hamilton advocated, had developed as an historical advance to protect the welfare of the population from local baronies, and foreign powers.[2] In a paper he wrote on Hamilton,[3] Roosevelt openly acknowledged Hamilton's critical role every step of the way in the formation of "a new and sturdier union" through the framing and ratification of the U.S. Constitution. He wrote:

> Washington, the first President under the Constitution, made Hamilton Secretary of the Treasury.... As he had stabilized the problems of State so now he ordered the finances of the country and it was his impetus that removed for all time the risk of disintegration of the States.

---

[2] Hunt, ed. *Ibid.*

[3] Anton Chaitkin, unpublished manuscript, "How Roosevelt Became a Revolutionary."

That's pretty strong praise. When FDR took office, the United States was once again threatened with disintegration. Private financial interests centered in Wall Street had acted so as to violate the population's basic rights to life, liberty, and the pursuit of happiness. In a 1932 speech to the San Francisco Commonwealth Club, candidate Roosevelt outlined his thought:

> Every man has a right to his own property; which means a right to be assured, to the fullest extent attainable, in the safety of his savings. By no other means can men carry the burdens of those parts of life which, in the nature of things afford no chance of labor; childhood, sickness, old age. In all thought of property, this right is paramount; all other property rights must yield to it. *If, in accord with this principle, we must restrict the operations of the speculator, the manipulator, even the financier, I believe we must accept the restriction as needful, not to hamper individualism but to protect it.*
>
> These two requirements must be satisfied, in the main, by the individuals who claim and hold control of the great industrial and financial combinations which dominate so large a part of our industrial life. They have undertaken

to be, not business men, but princes—princes of property. I am not prepared to say that the system which produces them is wrong. I am very clear that they must fearlessly and competently assume the responsibility which goes with the power. So many enlightened business men know this that the statement would be little more than a platitude, were it not for an added implication.

This implication is, briefly, that the responsible heads of finance and industry instead of acting each for himself, must work together to achieve the common end. They must, where necessary, sacrifice this or that private advantage; and in reciprocal self-denial must seek a general advantage. It is here that formal government—political government, if you choose, comes in. Whenever in the pursuit of this objective the lone wolf, the unethical competitor, the reckless promoter, the Ishmael or <u>Insull</u> whose hand is against every man's, declines to join in achieving an end recognized as being for the public welfare, and threatens to drag the industry back to a state of anarchy, the government may properly be asked to apply restraint.

> Likewise, should the group ever use
> its collective power contrary to public
> welfare, the government must be swift
> to enter and protect the public interest
> [emphasis added].[4]

After his election a few months later, FDR took on the responsibility to apply that restraint, some of which was eagerly sought by those bankers who could see that their greed had threatened to bring down the whole system. Thus, even before FDR could introduce the banking regulations against speculation ensconced in Glass-Steagall and the Securities Act, bankers such as Chase National Bank's Winthrop Aldrich[5] were campaigning for bank separation. (The major holdout remained London's favorite American banker, J.P. Morgan.)

But even after the FDR Administration had taken the initial steps to bring the banking system under control, Wall Street refused to direct funds into building up the economy; it continued to loot the population through foreclosures, refusing to adjust loans, and enforcing bankruptcies. FDR sought to deal with this sabotage by proposing that the Federal Reserve create

---

[4] Commonwealth Club address, September 23, 1932, American Rhetoric.com

[5] See Nomi Prins, *All the Presidents' Bankers, The Hidden Alliances That Drive American Power*, Nation Books, New York, 2014.

Hamiltonian "credit banks for industry,"[6] which would provide working capital to businesses which could not get it from Wall Street or other sources. When this effort failed, FDR and Reconstruction Finance Corporation (RFC) head Jesse Jones successfully moved to expand the Fed's authority to lend, and to pass the Industrial Advances Act of June 1934, which permitted the RFC to carry out the same functions FDR had proposed for the credit banks.

The 100 Days

FDR understood, as he said in his Inaugural Address, that his government had to "drive from the temple of our ancient faith those who had profaned it"—the "moneychangers in the temple"—and provide the basis for a government which would guarantee the security and peace necessary to the "pursuit of happiness."

While many Americans don't realize it today, the measures which FDR took in these first hundred days were literally matters of saving lives. Starvation faced millions of Americans who had been thrown off their land, out of their homes, or out of their jobs. People could not afford medical care, or food, or, in many cases, roofs over their heads. The private sector, and bankrupt local governments, were either throwing up

---

[6] Tim Sablik, "Fed Credit Policy during the Great Depression", Federal Reserve Bank of Richmond, March 2013, EB13-03. Click here.

their hands, or turning their backs. It was left to the Federal government to come to the rescue.

FDR applied Hamilton's principles of national banking to create millions of jobs, build infrastructure, and radically upgrade the U.S. economy. He undertook the task with the kind of "energy" which Hamilton had prescribed, first in the area of the financial system, and then in the areas of jobs and infrastructure. I will summarize each, before addressing how these measures fulfilled the commitments of the Constitution.

THE BANKING SYSTEM

FDR's first job, like Hamilton's, was to establish sovereign control over the banking system, and restore the public's trust.

When FDR took office in March 1933, he inherited a financial and political system which had been dominated, since the time of his cousin President Theodore Roosevelt (1901-08), by British economics. The axioms were those of British free enterprise, and the enforcer was the banking system, dominated by the Morgan-Mellon-du Pont interests.

The Morgan interests' control of credit gave them life-or-death control over the physical economy, and they were determined to use it to advance their own financial interests. Farms had been shut down *en masse*, while speculative schemes had flourished. Political favorites had gotten credit, whereas many productive enterprises received none and were forced to shut their doors.

These banking consortia worked in such a way as to deprive the United States of its sovereignty, through the enforcement of the British gold standard system, as it had done at the time Hamilton founded our system. The creation of credit was limited by the amount of gold held by the banks. Therefore, if the major banking interests decided to sell off their gold to buyers overseas, this resulted in a contraction of credit in the U.S. If the gold supply were controlled from overseas, as it effectively was, through the close-knit British-American banking establishment, then, the U.S. actually lacked sovereign control over its own currency and credit.[7]

To remedy this situation, FDR not only declared the famous Bank Holiday, but suspended all transactions in gold, and gave authority over any such matters to the Secretary of the Treasury. The Federal government got the authority to regulate the price of gold, rather than let that money-linked commodity be controlled by private interests.

On April 5, FDR went further, issuing an Executive Order against hoarding of gold. Historian Arthur Schlesinger described the significance of this move as follows:

> It meant that American monetary policy
> was no longer to be the quasi-automatic

---

[7] Note the similarity of this situation to that faced by Lincoln in the Civil War. See Chapter 5.

function of an international gold
standard; that it was to become instead
the instrument of conscious national
purpose.[8]

After removing gold as a weapon that could be used
by foreign or domestic institutions hostile to the welfare
of the nation, FDR still had to create the basis for a
national credit system that would serve the interests of
the nation.

The first point was clear: The banking system was
bankrupt. By calling the Bank Holiday on March 5,
Roosevelt dramatized this reality by ordering all banks
to be closed.

But then he had to put the system back together
again, which he did through the Emergency Banking
Act. This Act, which was rushed through Congress in
time to reopen the banks (or, most of them) on March
13, had various provisions for sorting the banks into
three classifications: those that were sound; those that
needed a capital infusion; and those which a conservator
would liquidate. It also permitted utilizing Federal
government instruments, like the Reconstruction
Finance Corporation and the Federal Reserve System,
to ensure that liquidity would be provided for those
banks that were basically sound, but needed it.

Upon passage of the Emergency Banking Act,
auditors from the Federal government were sent out

[8] Arthur Schlesinger, *The Age of Roosevelt, The Coming of the New
Deal*, Houghton Mifflin, Boston, 1965.

around the country to examine the banks' books. On the eve of the reopening, FDR gave his first Fireside Chat, when an estimated 60 million Americans heard him explain the measures he'd taken and how they had "nothing to fear but fear itself." The next day, a large majority of the more than 6,000 nationally chartered banks opened their doors, providing the basis for issuing payrolls, and maintaining government and other necessary social functions. Sufficient confidence had been restored, that the same citizens who had been carrying out runs on the banks, now put more money into the banking system in this period, than they took out.

A number of necessary complements to the audit came at the end of the 100 Days, including, most importantly, the Glass-Steagall Banking Act which separated commercial and investment banking, and established the Federal Deposit Insurance Corporation.

CREATING JOBS

Before the month of March was out, FDR turned his attention to the equally urgent question of creating jobs.

The first measure he took was the creation of the Civilian Conservation Corps (CCC), a government-administered program to create jobs, especially for unemployed youth. Over the course of its history, the CCC created more than *3 million* jobs, which permitted young men to support their families, and regain their health and morale, while doing something useful for the natural resources of the country.

This jobs program was followed later with the creation of public-works programs, which provided millions more with useful work, particularly in the repair and construction of infrastructure, such as waterworks, roads, and schools. Roosevelt's appointee Harry Hopkins personally embodied the spirit of these jobs programs as non-bureaucratic responses to the need for public improvements, as well as incomes. The Public Works Administration (PWA), established in the Summer of 1933, created hundreds of thousands of jobs, many of them building local infrastructure such as roads, water mains, parks, and the like.

Total estimates for the jobs created through these New Deal programs range as high as 20 million.[9] Over the course of his 12 years in office, FDR launched more than 45,000 projects in the five basic categories of infrastructure: water, power, transportation, health, and education. The Works Progress Administration (WPA) built more than 125,000 new buildings, including schools, public buildings, and libraries; 20,000 miles of water mains; 1,000 new or renovated airports; 600,000 miles of urban and rural roads, etc. CCC built 47,000 bridges, and 200 large dams, in addition to the massive reforestation it carried out. The Civil Works Administration (CWA) built 2,000 new levees, 9,000

---

[9] http://www.laboreducator.org/newdeal2.htm

miles of drainage and irrigation ditches, and 7,000 bridges. The PWA built 11,000 miles of streets, 388 new bridges, 384 airports, 2,000 complete waterworks, power plants, dams, and canals.

In addition to providing jobs, Roosevelt set up a national relief program, better known today as welfare, by which the Federal government shared the cost of supporting those families who did not have a breadwinner. In establishing this program, FDR explicitly rejected the idea that unemployment was the fault of the individual, and acknowledged that it was toleration of the rapacious system of cartels and economic royalists which created the hardships. Society had a responsibility, therefore, to care for the "least of these."

Other immediate measures for saving lives involved ending evictions from homes and farms. Millions found themselves without the ability to pay their mortgages, or to get credit to refinance. FDR recognized this as a national emergency, and intervened to provide the means for refinancing for those who were in desperate need.

While his opponents screamed "socialism," FDR could confidently scoff at them. He knew that his programs were providing the basis for putting the nation back to work and restoring the tax base. Every Federal works program created many corresponding jobs in the private sector which had to provide the materials. Every infrastructure improvement increased the potential for a productive, skilled workforce. While helping the poor, these programs demonstrably lifted the conditions of life for the entire nation—i.e., served the general welfare.

The Hoover Dam, a major project from FDR's "Four Quarters" infrastructure plan for the nation. (U.S. Bureau of Reclamation)

INFRASTRUCTURE

The third major element of the Hundred Days was creating transformative infrastructure, such as dams and hydroelectric plants. The flagship project was the Tennessee Valley Authority (TVA), a project long on the drawing boards, which FDR pushed through in May of 1933.

Major infrastructure projects, such as the Bonneville hydroelectric dam and the TVA, were conceived by Roosevelt not just as jobs programs, but as means of permanently upgrading the productivity of the economy and the productive powers of labor.[10] Such projects introduced the era of cheap electricity, and in many cases, provided the basis for conquering disease and ending the devastation of periodic floods. FDR knew that they would not pay for themselves in the short term, but would do so over the long-term, not just in terms of dollars and cents, but, most importantly, in terms of the standard of living of the entire nation.[11]

---

[10] FDR's approach was in line with that of Hamilton, who, along with Washington, Knox, and John Adams, fought to create an engineering corps and the West Point Academy, as assets for building the national infrastructure. West Point was finally founded in 1802.

[11] To learn the scope of the accomplishments of the TVA, click here, or read the official report of the TVA entitled "TVA, Its Work & Accomplishments, here.

EXERTING CONSTITUTIONAL AUTHORITY

Many have charged that the New Deal as a whole was a haphazard collection of measures, "pragmatically" intended to address the nation's crises. FDR himself argued to the contrary. In the introduction to Vol. II of his *Public Papers*, published in 1938, FDR encapsulated the New Deal as follows:

> The word "Deal" implies that the Government itself was going to use affirmative action to bring about its avowed objectives rather than stand by and hope that general economic laws alone would attain them. The word "New" implied that a new order of things designed to benefit the great mass of our farmers, workers and business would replace the old order of special privilege in a Nation which was completely and thoroughly disgusted with the existing dispensation.

> The New Deal was fundamentally intended as a modern expression of ideals set forth one hundred and fifty years ago in the Preamble of the Constitution of the United States–"a more perfect union, justice, domestic tranquility, the common defense, the general welfare

and the blessings of liberty to ourselves
and our posterity."

But we were not to be content with merely
hoping for these ideals. We were to use the
instrumentalities and powers of Government
actively to fight for them.[12] [emphasis
added]

As far as his banking measures were concerned,
FDR was following Hamilton: he had no question
but that the U.S. Constitution gives control over
the currency of the United States to the Federal
government, specifically Congress. Article I, Section
8 makes that clear. When this principle was challenged
in the early days of the Republic, the founding genius
of the American System of economics, Alexander
Hamilton, came forward to argue the case explicitly in
his Opinion on the Constitutionality of the National
Bank. (See Chapter 8)

Although FDR's banking measures never went so
far as to restore the National Bank, the President found
a way to exercise this sovereign power by other means,
especially through the Hamiltonian Reconstruction
Finance Corporation (see below).

As far as providing jobs for the population, FDR
could rely on the Constitutional commitment to

---

[12] Franklin Roosevelt, *The Public Papers and Addresses of Franklin*
D. Roosevelt, second volume, *The Year of Crisis, 1933,* Random
House, 1938.

using Federal power for the common good—what the Preamble to the Constitution calls the "general welfare." It was on this basis, that the President justified his far-flung initiatives for creating jobs, saving the farm sector, and establishing a safety net for those who had suffered from the "dog-eat-dog" economy which had predominated under the Tory ideas of Andrew Mellon, Calvin Coolidge, J.P. Morgan, and the like.

When two of his most ambitious long-term measures, the Social Security Act and unemployment insurance, were challenged in the courts, FDR's administration argued successfully that they were constitutional. "There was need of help from the nation if the people were not to starve," wrote Associate Justice Benjamin Cardozo in this decision. "It is too late today for the argument to be heard with tolerance that, in a crisis so extreme, the use of the moneys of the nation to relieve the unemployment and their dependents is a use for any purpose narrower than the promotion of the general welfare." At the same time, again citing the General Welfare clause, the Court upheld the old-age benefits provisions of the Social Security Act. In this case, *Helvering v. Davis*, Justice Cardozo expressly adopted the Hamiltonian view of the general welfare power, as opposed to that of Madison.

"The conception of the spending power advocated by Hamilton and strongly reinforced by Story has prevailed over that of Madison," Cardozo wrote. He said that in response to the nationwide calamity that began in 1929, Congress had enacted various measures conducive to the general welfare, including old-age benefits and unemployment compensation. Only a national, not a state, power can serve the interests of all, Cardozo declared.[13]

FDR's major infrastructure projects—especially the Four Quarters dam projects[14]—also followed the Hamiltonian tradition. All were conceived as major upgrades to the productivity of the national economy, by providing water management, power generation, and transportation. They were uniquely appropriate for national support due to their scope, and their long-term horizon in providing benefits for the population. They were indeed following the prescription of the Preamble that we provide not only for ourselves, but for our posterity.

These Hamiltonian policies created what even today is called the "Golden Age of Productivity" in the U.S. economy, a rate of growth of Total Factor Productivity[15] of over 3% per year going into the 1950s.[16] That figure compares to a level of under 1% today.

---

[13] These decisions are cited in a May 15, 2000 article in *The New Federalist* by Edward Spannaus, entitled "What is the `General Welfare?'" It can be found here on the web (http://american_almanac.tripod.com/welfare.htm)

[14] These were the St. Lawrence Seaway in the Northeast, the TVA in the Southeast, the Boulder (later Hoover) Dam of the Colorado River in the Southwest, and the Columbia River dams in the Northwest.

[15] See Glossary.

[16] See Nancy Spannaus, "The FDR Model: The "Golden Age" of Productivity," at americansystemnow. com. Click here.

The commitment to improving nature and society for the benefit of future generations has become increasingly foreign to our national philosophy, since the 1960s Counterculture and the "me" generation. There used to be a joke in the 1970s, that whereas the Japanese businessman planned for six years ahead, the U.S. businessman planned for six minutes, this being the amount of time that it could take for stocks to be traded on the relevant gambling exchanges. In today's computer age, it would appear that the attention span has contracted further, to perhaps six seconds.

THE HAMILTONIAN RECONSTRUCTION FINANCE CORPORATION

Much of the funding for the New Deal infrastructure came from the Reconstruction Finance Corporation (RFC), which had been created by the Hoover Administration. FDR used the RFC as a national bank.[17] It was funded through the Treasury but functioned as a bank. It had revolving fund lending capabilities, was directed to infrastructure and industrial projects only, and had the independence to intervene directly into the physical economy. In conjunction with the Federal government, it became the largest source of credit in the economy. It also became the largest U.S. bank by

---

[17] For a comprehensive history of the RFC under Jesse Jones, see Steven Fenberg, *Unprecedented Power, Jesse Jones, Capitalism and the Common Good*, Houston Endowment, Inc., 2011, 550 pp.

far, and by 1940 was known as "the fourth branch of government."

During the New Deal, the RFC deployed between $15 and $20 billion into the recovery effort. It gave WPA $1 billion at its founding to start public works projects, and another $2 billion loan over time. The RFC took over the municipal bonds held by the PWA and sold them on the markets to raise capital for the public works projects. The RFC directly helped fund the Hoover Dam, Grand Coulee Dam, the Bonneville Dam, and the Mississippi flood control projects.

From 1933-1939, 70% of the new school buildings and 35% of the hospitals were funded by the RFC. The funding was done on the basis of long-term 5 to 20-year loans at very low interest rates, and ultimately, virtually all loans were repaid.

The RFC was crucial to reviving housing financing. It set up the Home Owners Loan Corporation (HOLC) with $200 million for its capital stock, and the HOLC ultimately refinanced 20% of all home mortgages. RFC gave the Federal Housing Administration (FHA) $200 million for its capital, and the RFC created the Federal National Mortgage Association (Fannie Mae) to finance mortgages. Fannie Mae became the main purchaser of FHA mortgages.

The RFC also intervened to aid the farm economy, which, at that time, was the largest sector of the nation, and mired in deep depression. The key agency that supported decent prices for farm commodities was the Commodity Credit Corporation, which was created in

1933. It was entirely funded by the RFC and allowed farmers to borrow money based on their crop output, valued at a much higher price. In 1933, the Commodity Credit Corporation had a lending capability of $1 billion backstopped by the RFC to save the farm sector.

The RFC was involved in many other farm projects, including the Rural Electric Administration. This agency brought electric power to rural America, created the electric cooperatives, and built the power lines. The Rural Electric Administration was almost entirely funded by the RFC.

During the New Deal period, virtually all RFC loans were repaid.

During World War II,[18] the RFC created numbers of subsidiaries including the Defense Plant Corporation (DPC), Metals Reserve Corporation, Rubber Reserve Corporation (RRC), and Defense Supplies Corporation (DSC). The RFC-generated DPC built the entire machine-tool industry during this period, spending nearly $2 billion to create an industry that was state of the art, and deploying tools into newly built factories.

The DPC was at the center of building a military airplane industry virtually from scratch. It funded the construction of new, assembly line, war plane factories (including the gigantic Willow Run plant in Detroit). It also built most of the engine companies. Fourteen of the 15 engine plants that supplied the modern engines to the planes were funded by DPC.

---

[18] See "Lessons for a Recovery: The WWII Economic Mobilization," by Stuart Rosenblatt, on https://americansystemnow.com

Without the crucial role of FDR's National Bank (i.e., the RFC) the ability to wage and win World War II would have been severely crippled or non-existent.

And again, virtually all of the loans generated by the RFC war industries were repaid or written off, and the agency[19] either broke even or turned a profit. All of this was due to the rapid increase in productivity in the entire economy and the generation of real wealth. From 1940-1945 Gross Domestic Product increased at over 10% per year, and productivity grew at 3-5% per year, rates[20] that have not been achieved since.

This never could have happened if the United States had followed the path recommended by Adam Smith, whose anti-American views we will now look at in more detail.

---

[19] The Final Report of the Reconstruction Finance Corporation, available on Fraser, Discover Economic History, Federal Reserve.

[20] See Stuart Rosenblatt's review of "The American `Special Century' of Economic Progress, 1870-1970," on https://americansystemnow.com

Adam Smith, as portrayed by his statue in Edinburgh, Scotland (stock.adobe.com)

CHAPTER 7

Alexander Hamilton was a vigorous opponent of Adam Smith.

Not only wealth, but the independence and security of a Country, appear to be materially connected with the prosperity of manufactures. Every nation, with a view to those great objects, ought to endeavor to possess within itself all the essentials of national supply. These comprise the means of Subsistence, habitation, clothing, *and* defence [emphasis in the original].

−*Report on Manufactures*

WHY RETURN TO the question of Adam Smith? Because a concerted campaign has led many to believe the lie that his ideas contribute to the growth of the American economy.

Much has been made of the fact that British political economist Smith's tome *The Wealth of Nations*[1] was published in 1776, the same year as the Declaration of Independence. It is not unusual to find commentators insinuating coherence between the impetus behind Smith's demand for freedom of the markets, and the American colonists' demand for freedom from the tyranny of the British Crown. This fallacy has been further reinforced in the ideological counterattack against FDR's Hamiltonian measures which began in the late 1940s, when the Austrian School of Friedrich von Hayek and Ludwig von Mises launched a huge campaign[2] in favor of Smithian "free enterprise" as the American way, a campaign which continues today.

In reality, Smith was just a spokesman for a faction of the British Empire, which, despite differences with the British Crown over methods, was determined to maintain the American colonies as its looting ground. Some American patriots, such as James Madison, were taken in by his arguments, but not Alexander

---

[1] The full name is *An Inquiry into the Nature and Causes of the Wealth of Nations.*

[2] Friedrich von Hayek established the Mt. Pelerin Society in 1947 to counter dirigist economic policies like FDR's. Among his leading targets was American System economist Friedrich List. Since then, von Hayek devotees have sponsored dozens of institutes which promote Adam Smith as the hero of economic freedom. Among them are the Heritage Foundation and the Adam Smith Institute.

Hamilton.[3] As he showed in his *Report on Manufactures*, and I discussed at length in Chapter 3, Hamilton knew that Smith's advocacy of free trade was a prescription for maintaining British control over the United States. To defend the gains of the Revolution, Hamilton put forward the American System.

Hamilton's criticism of Smith on the question of whether the United States should actively promote manufactures was not simply a tactical dispute. It reflected the fundamental difference between Hamilton's conception of economy, and that of imperial apologist Smith: an industrial republic vs. an imperial satrapy, the American System vs. the British System.[4]

SMITH VERSUS AMERICA

Adam Smith's views against American industrialization were laid out plainly in *The Wealth of Nations*. He wrote in Vol. 1, Book II, Chapter V:

> Were the Americans, either by combination or by any other sort of violence, to stop the importation of European manufactures, and, by thus

---

[3] See Samuel Fleischacker, "Adam Smith's Reception among the American Founders, 1776-1790", *The William and Mary Quarterly,* Vol. 59, No. 4 (Oct, 2002), pp. 897-924 (28 pages). Click here.

[4] Henry Carey's elaboration on this distinction is worth re-reading. See Chapter 5.

giving a monopoly to such of their own
countrymen as could manufacture the
like goods, divert any considerable part
of their capital into this employment,
they would retard instead of accelerating
the further increase in the value of their
annual produce, and would obstruct
instead of promoting the progress of
their country towards real wealth and
greatness.

Really? Was continued dependence upon European
(mostly British) manufactures, and continued reliance
on raw materials exports to Europe, really the path to
progress? Smith knew it was not. Like his sponsor Lord
Shelburne, he was willing to go so far as to advocate
American independence, as long as the new country
could be convinced to maintain its proper economic
subservience within the Empire.

As he shows in his *Report on Manufactures*, Hamilton
knows Smith's argument is an outright lie: England itself
did not develop its industrial and commercial strength
without government direction, and neither could the
young United States. Unfortunately, we do not have
the document which Hamilton's son John Church
Hamilton claims he wrote in the 1780s critiquing
Smith.[5] But Hamilton's *Report on Manufactures* functions
as a fulsome refutation of Smith's argument. Hamilton

---

[5] John C. Hamilton, *Life of Alexander Hamilton, a History of the
Republic of the United States of America* (Boston, 1879), II, 514.

quotes extensively from the British imperialist at the beginning of the *Report*, although not by name. This is the argument of opponents of manufactures, he says, putting quotation marks around it:

> "To endeavor by the extraordinary patronage of Government, to accelerate the growth of manufactures, is in fact, to endeavor, by force and art, to transfer the *natural current* of industry, from a more, to a less beneficial channel. Whatever has such a tendency must necessarily be unwise. Indeed it can hardly ever be wise in a government, to attempt to give a direction to the industry of its citizens. This under the quicksighted guidance of private interest, will, if left to itself, infallibly find its own way to the most profitable employment: and 'tis by such employment, that the public prosperity will be most effectually promoted. To leave industry to itself, therefore, is, in almost every case, the soundest as well as the simplest policy.

> "This policy is not only recommended to the United States, by considerations which affect all nations, it is, in a manner, dictated to them by the imperious force of a very peculiar situation. The

smallness of their population compared with their territory—the constant allurements to emigration from the settled to the unsettled parts of the country—the facility, with which the less independent condition of an artisan can be exchanged for the more independent condition of a farmer, these and similar causes conspire to produce, and for a length of time must continue to occasion, a scarcity of hands for manufacturing occupation, and dearness of labor generally. To these disadvantages for the prosecution of manufactures, a deficiency of pecuniary capital being added, the prospect of a successful competition with the manufactures of Europe must be regarded as little less than desperate. Extensive manufactures can only be the offspring of a redundant, at least of a full population. Till the latter shall characterise the situation of this country, 'tis vain to hope for the former.

"If contrary to the *natural course of things*, an unseasonable and premature spring can be given to certain fabrics, by heavy duties, prohibitions, bounties, or by other forced expedients; this will only be to sacrifice the interests of the community to those of particular classes. Besides the misdirection of labour, a virtual monopoly will be given to the persons employed on such fabrics; and an enhancement of price, the inevitable consequence of every monopoly, must be defrayed at the expence of the other parts of the society. It is far preferable, that those persons should be engaged in the cultivation of the earth, and that we should procure, in exchange for its productions, the commodities, with which foreigners are able to supply us in greater perfection, and upon better terms. [emphasis added]"

The whole of Hamilton's following *Report* is devoted to countering Smith's assertions, theoretically and practically, as my earlier review demonstrates.[6]

For the United States to wait until the "natural course of things" leads to the development of manufactures, Hamilton argues, would mean that the young country, then primarily an agricultural nation and a supplier of raw materials to other nations, remains totally dependent upon foreign demand for its products. This is a "precarious reliance," Hamilton argues, and thus the best policy is to rely on the domestic market and build that market by fostering the development of manufactures.

---

[6] See Chapter 2.

Hamilton directly addresses Smith's contention as follows:

> If the system of perfect liberty to industry and commerce were the prevailing system of nations—the arguments which dissuade a country in the predicament of the United States, from the zealous pursuits of manufactures would doubtless have great force. It will not be affirmed, that they might not be permitted, with few exceptions, to serve as a rule of national conduct. In such a state of things, each country would have the full benefit of its peculiar advantages to compensate for its deficiencies or disadvantages. If one nation were in condition to supply manufactured articles on better terms than another, that other might find an abundant indemnification in a superior capacity to furnish the produce of the soil. And a free exchange, mutually beneficial, of the commodities which each was able to supply, on the best terms, might be carried on between them, supporting in full vigour the industry of each. And though the circumstances which have been mentioned and others, which will be unfolded hereafter

render it probable, that nations merely Agricultural would not enjoy the same degree of opulence, in proportion to their numbers, as those which united manufactures with agriculture; yet the progressive improvement of the lands of the former might, in the end, atone for an inferior degree of opulence in the mean time: and in a case in which opposite considerations are pretty equally balanced, the option ought perhaps always to be, in favour of leaving Industry to its own direction.

But the system which has been mentioned, is far from characterising the general policy of Nations. [The prevalent one has been regulated by an opposite spirit.][7]

The consequence of it is, that the United States are to a certain extent in the situation of a country precluded from foreign Commerce. They can indeed, without difficulty obtain from abroad the manufactured supplies,

---

[7] The brackets around this sentence are not explained in the most recent republications of the Report, as in founders. archives.gov., or the Syrett-edited *Collected Papers of Alexander Hamilton*. Earlier reprints, as in the 1964 Harper Torchbook edition edited by Jacob E. Cooke, do not include brackets.

of which they are in want; but they experience numerous and very injurious impediments to the emission and vent of their own commodities. Nor is this the case in reference to a single foreign nation only. The regulations of several countries, with which we have the most extensive intercourse, throw serious obstructions in the way of the principal staples of the United States.

In such a position of things, the United States cannot exchange with Europe on equal terms; and the want of reciprocity would render them the victim of a system, which should induce them to confine their views to Agriculture and refrain from Manufactures. *A constant and encreasing necessity, on their part, for the commodities of Europe, and only a partial and occasional demand for their own, in return, could not but expose them to a state of impoverishment, compared with the opulence to which their political and natural advantages authorise them to aspire.* [emphasis added]

Hamilton sees through Smith's smokescreen of concern for America achieving wealth and greatness. Smith's policy is a path to impoverishment for Americans, he says, and he is right.

The British Empire's centuries-long looting of India, especially by the British East India Company, not only kept it impoverished, but led to periodic famines. Here, we see Indians scavenging for subsistence in garbage dumps. (stock.adobe.com)

FREE TRADE EQUALS GENOCIDE

Under the most extreme interpretation of Smith's economic theory, a national government is consigned to passivity, as individual producers and consumers pursue their own (largely financial) interests, the result of which is expected to be positive for society as a whole. In fact, Smith did not oppose all government intervention—he supported taxation, some government investment in vital infrastructure, and the like for Great Britain—but he propounded the idea that government direction of the economy (including setting major economic goals) was generally destructive and should be avoided. This was particularly to be applied to the colonies, who might otherwise try to challenge control by the mother country.

Smith was a close colleague, and perhaps an outright tool,[8] the British aristocrat Lord Shelburne (William Petty), a "liberal" who opposed trying to control the American colonies by use of military force; he headed the British government during the 1783 peace negotiations. Shelburne, like William Pitt the Younger (British prime minister between 1783 and 1801), proposed that Great Britain keep America, in particular, within the imperial fold through a policy of free trade. Smith was their "theoretician," or apologist, for this policy.

In theory, as Smith defined it, free trade would be governed by the "natural order" of a nation's physical endowments and advantages. Therefore, according to his system, colonies such as America and India should stick to producing raw materials for the mother country and importing the manufactured goods they needed. It would be against the "natural order" for such countries, lacking the machinery and domestic capital to produce as efficiently as England, to attempt to provide manufactured goods for themselves.

---

[8] For a fascinating review of their relationship, see "Before Hegemony: Adam Smith, American Independence, and the Origins of the First Era of Globalization," by James Ashley Morris, *International Organization*, vol. 66, no. 3 (Summer 2012), pp. 395–428 https://www.jstor.org/stable/23279962

In reality, free trade was the brutal imposition of looting and impoverishment, enforced, when necessary, by the use of military might.

One instrumentality for imposing that force in the late 18th and early 19th century was the British East India Company, a private corporation set up in 1600 as a monopoly for trade with the East. By the mid-1700s the Company was well-known for its major role in the slave trade, and its virtual rape of Asian countries such as India. This reputation became even more notorious after the 1770 Famine of Bengal, in which an estimated *ten million Indians* died as a result of its policies.[9] The Company had been granted total authority over the finances and government of the region by the British government, which it applied ruthlessly.

News of the horrors caused by the famine spread widely in the American colonies, with first-hand accounts of bodies littering the streets.[10] It didn't take much imagination for Americans to fear a similar future if they were subjected to the policies of that company, which had the backing of the British Crown and parliament. Recall that the Tea Act of 1773 gave the East India Company a monopoly on the sale of tea in the American colonies, including the right to collect taxes on tea. The spectre of Bengal in America was not far-fetched.

---

[9] For a good source on the British looting of India, see Amartya Sen, "Imperial Illusions," *The New Republic*, Dec. 31, 2007.

[10] See https://americansystemnow.com/the-1770-indian-famine-and-the-american-revolution/.

Smith promoter Lord Shelburne was a major stockholder in the East India Company.[11] And while his protégé Smith was on record criticizing the governmental powers given to the East India Company, he also considered its trading functions a "great service to the state."[12] And the refusal of the British to send grain to Bengal after the harvest failed and the famine broke out, cohered with Smith's *laissez-faire* policy.

Indeed, the result of British domination of the Indian economy resulted in no increase in India's per capita income from 1757 to 1947[13], and an estimated $45 trillion worth of wealth being extracted from that nation between 1765 and 1938.[14] Hamilton was determined that the young United States not suffer the same fate.

WHAT IS VALUE?

There is a serious theoretical divergence between Smith and Hamilton, in addition to the practical one. What is the actual source of value, or wealth, in an economy? The *Report on Manufactures* treats this issue

---

[11] See http://quod.lib.umich.edu/c/clementsmss/umich–wcl–M–66she?view=text

[12] Smith, Wealth of Nations on Multinationals.

[13] Mike Davis, *Late Victorian Holocausts: El Nino Famines and the Making of the Third World*, London, Verso Books, 2001.

[14] See *Agrarian and Other Histories, Essays for Binay Bhushan Chaudhuri* by Shubkra Chakrabarti and Utsa Patnail, Tulika Books, 2018.

extensively, and its argument, which I reviewed in Chapter 2, bears repeating in this context.

According to Hamilton, Smith had argued that, while manufacturing was a productive use of labor, the productivity of agriculture was superior to it. Hamilton tears huge holes in Smith's assertion, arguing that man's labor, through skill and art and the application of mechanical powers, is a major source of productivity. Hamilton also argues that "manufactures open a wider field to exertions of ingenuity than agriculture," and that its production can be more constant and dependable than agriculture, which depends upon the weather.

Although Hamilton does not maintain that manufacturing is more productive than agriculture, he insists that one cannot assert the superiority of agriculture alone. He sets out to demonstrate that "the establishment and diffusion of manufactures have the effect of rendering the total mass of useful and productive labor, in a community, *greater than it would otherwise be.*" [emphasis in the original] In other words, the development of an agro-industrial economy (inclusive of a commitment to increase those "mechanical powers" or technological progress mentioned above) is the pathway to "a positive augmentation of the total produce and revenue of the Society."

Later on, Hamilton becomes more polemical, directly taking on Smith's assertion that "industry, if left to itself, will naturally find its way to the most useful and profitable employment: whence it is inferred that manufactures without the aid of government will grow up as soon and as fast, as the natural state of things and the interest of the community may require."

Smith's argument is what is generally referred to as the "invisible hand," which he advances in Vol. I, Book IV, Chapter II of the *Wealth of Nations* as follows:

> But the annual revenue of every society is always precisely equal to the exchangeable value of the whole annual produced [sic] of its industry, or rather is precisely the same thing with that exchangeable value. As every individual, therefore, endeavours as much as he can both to employ his capital in the support of domestic industry, and so to direct that industry that its produce may be of the greatest value; every individual necessarily labours to render the annual revenue of the society as great as he can. *He generally, indeed, neither intends to promote the public interest, nor knows how much he is promoting it.* By preferring the support of domestic to that of foreign industry, he intends only his own gain, and he is in this, as in many other cases, led by an *invisible hand* to promote an end which was no part of his intention. Nor is it always the worse for the society that it was no part of it. By pursuing his own interest he frequently promotes

that of the society more effectually than
when he really intends to promote it...
[emphasis added]

The fallacies in this statement are many, starting with the assertion that value in the society is determined by its ability to be exchanged on the marketplace. This is the argument of those today who value a money-based, or purely market-based (the ability to buy cheaply and sell dear) economy, in preference to increasing value by developing the productive powers of labor. In reality, value is determined by the contributions a product makes to the progress of society as a whole.

Hamilton's view of money was not its purchasing power, and certainly not any intrinsic value, but rather that it provide a stable basis for investment in the economy.[15] He was concerned with creating markets for the productive output of farms and industries as a means of expanding and improving the economy.

The German economist Friedrich List, in his *Outlines of American Political Economy* (1827), encapsulates the difference between the Smithian view and that of Hamilton's American System most succinctly when he writes that the Smith system is oriented to gaining matter, i.e. material things, "in exchanging matter for matter," whereas the American System is geared to increasing the "productive power" of the nation. (Letter 4) Thus an economy based on obtaining its necessities cheaply (i.e. free trade) is the antithesis of one which

---

[15] Michael O'Malley, op. cit., pp. 122-123.

develops its own *powers* to produce those necessities (and thus maintains its independence).[16]

Recall that Hamilton argues that the United States is well-positioned to rapidly develop its manufacturing capability, due to "the late improvements to the employment of Machines, which substituting the Agency of fire and water, had prodigiously lessened the necessity of manual labour," the immigration of skilled labor, and the natural endowments of the country.

Overall, Hamilton's *Report* asserts that it is the deliberate increasing of the productive powers of labor through technology, improvements in infrastructure, and the use of government power to create credit that will produce value in the economy. Those who followed him in promoting the American System pursued that policy, and excoriated Adam Smith's policy of free trade.[17]

---

[16] Friedrich List, *ibid*.

[17] One of the most famous attacks on the fraud of the British trade system was a three-day oration by Sen. Henry Clay, given Feb. 2, 3, and 6 in 1832. Click here.

First Bank of the United States, Philadelphia, Pa.
(courtesy of Nancy Spannaus)

CHAPTER 8

Alexander Hamilton's banking system was not British!

This restrictive interpretation of the word necessary is also contrary to this sound maxim of construction namely, that the powers contained in a constitution of government, especially those which concern the general administration of the affairs of a country, its finances, trade, defence & ought to be construed liberally, in advancement of the public good. [emphasis added]

—Opinion on the Constitutionality of the National Bank

HAMILTON'S VISION OF a thriving agro-industrial economy depended upon having a reliable source of government-regulated credit. This was one of the crucial missions of his National Bank.

Thus, one of the most disorienting and vicious charges against Hamilton and his financial plan is the claim that he was adopting the British System.[1] This charge is often justified by Hamilton's explicit citation of the usefulness of the Bank of England in building the industrial power of the mother country, and his copying of various organizational features of that British bank in his schema for the Bank of the United States. As a few Hamilton scholars such as Forrest McDonald[2] and Donald Swanson[3] point out, this claim is a lie.

---

[1] The charge originated with the Jeffersonians in 1792, when the Secretary of State, in a rage about the establishment of the National Bank, began a newspaper campaign charging that Hamilton's bank was part of his desire to establish a British monarchy in America. He cited Hamilton's speech at the Constitutional Convention and comments Hamilton allegedly made at the dinner where he, Jefferson, and James Madison made the deal to pass the Assumption bill, in exchange for moving the U.S. Capital to the South. Hamilton rebutted the charges, among other places, in an Aug. 18, 1792 letter to George Washington, where he noted that the promoters of anarchy are the "true Artificers of Monarchy." Given Hamilton's lifelong fight to establish and defend the republican U.S. Constitution, the charges of his being a monarchist are worse than absurd.

[2] Forrest McDonald, *Alexander Hamilton, A Biography*, W.W. Norton & Company, New York, 1979, *passim*.

[3] Donald F. Swanson, "Origins of Hamilton's Fiscal Policies," University of Florida Monographs, *Social Sciences*, No. 17, Winter 1963, *passim*.

A NATIONAL VISION

The first fundamental difference between the two banks lies in the *purpose* for which they were created. Hamilton's Bank of the United States was intended as one means of creating the "more perfect union" which the Preamble to the U.S. Constitution had called for, by establishing a central sovereign currency, banking system, and source of *credit* to build the nation. It was a cornerstone for nation-building. By contrast, the Bank of England was established in 1694 as a means of amassing funding for the Crown's plans for war against France.

Hamilton's writings, from as early as 1774, demonstrate that he had a vision for creating a large commercial republic, in which the widely differing regions of the nation would complement each other in producing a growing economy. This vision emphasized the development of increasing mechanization, creation of a manufacturing base, and urbanization. These economic characteristics were incompatible with the continuation of the slave-based economy that Great Britain had brought to the United States.

Hamilton's personal actions in opposition to slavery, especially with the New York Manumission Society, and the establishment of the <u>African Free School</u> to educate the children of slaves,[4] are not the only evidence that he sought an end to that institution. Best known is his proposal, with John Laurens, to

---

[4] See Introduction.

bring slaves into the Revolutionary Army (along with giving them their freedom). But most importantly, his financial system, with its orientation to building up the productive powers of labor and nation-unifying infrastructure, and undercutting the power of the landed oligarchy, represented a mortal threat to the slave system. For this reason, the slave-holding oligarchy and its financiers understood and feared Hamilton's system, and determined to co-opt or outright destroy it.

To accomplish his vision, Hamilton devised an ingenious plan that would turn what appeared to be a crushing debt burden (the foreign, continental, and state debts incurred during the Revolution, which amounted to $77 million, an enormous sum at the time), into a source of credit and capital which could be used to invest in developing the nation. When he took over the Treasury, the United States was hopelessly behind in interest payments, and the revenues which would be available from the tariff (passed in August of 1789) would not even cover the debt service, much less suffice for the government's expenses. Without the development of a productive economy, there was no prospect these debts ever could be paid.

Hamilton's solution was 1) to increase the Federal debt burden by assuming the state debts; 2) to reorganize that debt into new government bonds; and 3) to utilize those bonds to capitalize a national bank which would fund investments in the economy. This would effectively turn debt into credit for the real economy. Unlike those who wanted to pay off or cancel the debt right away, he insisted on putting it to work to increase the productive powers of the nation. Bond- and stock-holders would be paid their annual rates of interest, but would have to be in it for the long haul, as any investment in the physical development of a nation has to be.

It boggled the minds of many Americans, and still does to this day, that Hamilton chose to *increase* the Federal debt, but his purposes were critical for the unity of the nation. He argued in the *First Report on Public Credit* (January 9, 1790) that the debts of the war were the responsibility of the entire country, as it was the entire country which benefited from their being incurred. By consolidating the debt, he aimed at further consolidating the 13 former colonies into one nation. As he wrote in 1781 to financier Robert Morris:

> A national debt, if it is not too excessive,
> will be to us a national blessing. It will
> be a powerful cement of our union.[5]

As for those who wanted to cancel the debt, or cut it substantially, Hamilton considered them short-sighted, as well as immoral. Honoring the war debts of the past, he understood, could provide the basis for creating prosperity for the future.

Hamilton was out to establish public credit for the sake of the nation as a whole. For this, he has often been accused of wanting to maintain the debt for the purpose of enriching the nation's creditors, or the power of the

---

[5] Letter to Robert Morris, April 30, 1781.

Federal government *per se*. He wanted nothing of the kind. In that *First Report*, he asserted that

> Persuaded as the Secretary is, that the proper funding of the present debt, will render it a national blessing: Yet he is so far from acceding to the position, in the latitude in which it is sometimes laid down, that "public debts are public benefits," a position inviting to prodigality, and liable to dangerous abuse,—that he ardently wishes to see it incorporated, as a fundamental maxim, in the system of public credit of the United States, that the creation of debt should always be accompanied with the means of extinguishment. This he regards as the true secret for rendering public credit immortal.

Unlike many others, however, Hamilton understood that providing the means of "extinguishment" meant more than guaranteeing a revenue stream for interest payments; it required increasing the productive powers of the nation. That is a long-term process, which requires investment in infrastructure, skills, and innovation. Thus, the need for *credit* to generate that productive activity.

What a contrast to the short-term profit-taking and budget-balancing of today!

CREATING A STABLE CURRENCY

The second major difference between Hamilton's banking system and the Bank of England flowed from the first: while the Bank of England was chartered to be an instrument of government policy, and was capitalized exclusively by public debt, Hamilton devised the Bank of the United States to be operated as a quasi-private, profit-making institution. He did not want the Bank to be piggy bank for the government, but a commercial bank.

Stock purchases had to be made three-quarters in public debt, but the rest had to be paid in specie. Yes, the Federal government owned 20% of the stock, and the bank charter specified the right of the Secretary of the Treasury to inspect its books, require statements of account, and remove the government's deposits at any time. *But the BUS was prohibited from trading in government bonds!* It was not allowed to speculate in the credit of the United States or buy government debt to finance wars or other misadventures, as was the Bank of England.

The BUS rendered vital services to the Federal government. It acted as a depository for government funds, issued bank notes which would provide a large, secure money supply for the country, facilitated the payment of taxes, and served as a source for short-term loans. The circulation of bank paper that could be used anywhere in the nation greatly increased efficient and profitable trade between regions of the nation, and thus the productivity of the economy. The BUS notes served as a national currency, gradually supplanting the mish-mash of Spanish, Dutch, and British coin, not to mention the various local bank paper, which was being used throughout the nation.

The Bank of England in London (stock.adobe.com)

COMMERCIAL OPERATIONS

The third major difference lay in the role which the two banks played in commercial operations. For the Bank of England, any commercial operations were strictly subordinate to its primary function as an instrument of the government. The Bank of England was to provide funds for government activities, but, in effect, its investors held power over the government by dictating what activities it would and would not fund. To the contrary, the BUS, as Hamilton so eloquently expressed in his *Second Report on Public Credit*, was intended to use the backing of public credit (the government bonds which made up the bulk of its capitalization) to provide credit for enhancing the productive activity of the country in agriculture, manufacturing, and commerce.

This difference of intention is vital, and reflects Hamilton's reliance on a totally different concept of political economy than that of Great Britain. McDonald's succinct summary makes this clear:

> ...Hamilton's system was erected upon the same three institutions as the British system—funding, a national bank, and a sinking fund. But the resemblance was largely superficial, for Hamilton founded the institutions on different principles and used them in different ways to obtain different ends. The British system was designed solely as a means of raising money for purposes of government; political, social and economic by-products of the system, though profound, were incidental.

> Hamilton's system was designed to
> employ financial means to achieve
> political, economic, and social ends;
> and that made all the difference in the
> world.[6]

While Hamilton clearly was a genius in devising the Federal government's financial institutions to create a nation out of bankruptcy and chaos, he did have models other than the Bank of England to work from.

Fundamental Principles

Hamilton never wrote an autobiographical account of the evolution of his thinking on banking, so we are left to discover them indirectly.

Hamilton's readings in economic theory and history were voluminous, and only partially documented. His pay books during the Revolutionary War indicate that he read and studied Malachi Postlethwayt's *Universal Dictionary of Trade and Commerce* and many other British economic writers like Richard Price and Wyndham Beawes. These he combined with readings in political theory, especially David Hume. But he also read extensively about continental political economy, from which he became familiar with the ideas of the Swiss philosopher-jurist Emmerich Vattel, the French Minister of Finance Jean-Baptiste Colbert, the Scottish

---

[6] McDonald, *ibid.*, p. 161.

financier John Law, and Louis XVI's Finance Minister Jacques Neckar. It is from the latter group, especially Colbert and Vattel, that Hamilton found the most useful concepts for *nation-building*.

Hamilton's view of Colbert comes into view in his *Continentalist* papers, written in 1782 as part of his campaign for moving the country from the Confederation to a true Union. In the fifth of that series, Hamilton wrote:

> Trade may be said to have taken its rise in England under the auspices of Elizabeth; and its rapid progress there is in a great measure to be ascribed to the fostering care of government in that and succeeding reigns.
>
> From a different spirit in the government, with superior advantages, France was much later in commercial improvements, nor would her trade have been at this time in so prosperous a condition had it not been for the abilities and indefatigable endeavors of the great Colbert. He laid the foundation of the French commerce, and taught the way to his successors to enlarge and improve it. The establishment of the woolen manufacture, in a kingdom, where nature seemed to have denied the means,

is one among many proofs, how much may be effected in favor of commerce by the attention and patronage of a wise administration. The number of useful edicts passed by Louis XIV, and since his time, in spite of frequent interruptions from the jealous enmity of Great Britain, has advanced that of France to a degree which has excited the envy and astonishment of its neighbors.

As historian Christopher White pointed out in *The Political Economy of the American Revolution*,[7] Colbert used his period as Finance Minister for Louis XIV (1663-1683) to break France free of its financial thralldom to the Dutch Empire, and build it into a unified, productive nation. Colbert's measures—building road and canal infrastructure, establishing a system of centralized taxation free of feudal interference, creating a flourishing wool industry through tariffs and subsidies, and erecting lasting, effective fortifications against attack, to name a few—stemmed from his anti-monetarist concept of what constitutes wealth. For him, wealth was not amassing silver and gold, but the continuous expansion of the productive powers of the nation and its population.

---

[7] Christopher White, "Jean-Baptiste Colbert and the Origins of Industrial Capitalism," in *The Political Economy of the American Revolution*, Nancy Spannaus and Christopher White, eds., second edition, *EIR*, 1995, pp. 53-106.

That Colbert understood that these productive powers came from the development of science and the human mind, is demonstrated by the fact that the Royal Academy which he created sponsored such outstanding scientists as Christiaan Huyghens and Gottfried Leibniz.

A comparison of this brief outline of Colbert's policies with those developed by our First Treasury Secretary, in both the *Report on the National Bank* and the *Report on Manufactures*, underscores the coherence of their thought.

The Swiss philosopher-jurist Emmerich Vattel (1714-1767) also looms large as a major continental influence on Hamilton's thinking, as well as that of other founding fathers. Having adopted the philosophical outlook of Gottfried Leibniz, Vattel became a major publicist for a Leibnizian view of statecraft, which he elaborated in his 1758 book *The Law of Nations*.[8] That book arrived in the United States in 1762 and was widely circulated among leading nationalist circles, finally becoming the most cited work in legal cases into the 19th Century. McDonald says that Hamilton read it in 1782.

Vattel's work develops a concept of national sovereignty based on his view of natural law, by which he meant the laws of nature. Vattel considered the fundamental axiom of natural law to be that "the great end of every being endowed with intellect and sentiment, is happiness." (See Introduction for

---

[8] Vattel's *Law of Nations* has been reprinted in English by The Liberty Fund, Indianapolis, 2008.

comparison with Hamilton) He then defined the true purposes of good government as to provide for the nation's necessities, to "procure the true happiness" of the nation, and to fortify the nation against external attacks. For Vattel, a sovereign government must play an active role in securing these aims, which contrast sharply with the governmental aims defined by the British empiricist philosophers (e.g., John Locke)— preserving the individual's right to life, liberty, and property.

McDonald emphasizes the similarity between the aims of Hamilton's political economy, and those of Vattel. He believes Hamilton evolved beyond his earlier adherence to Humean cynicism.[9] In addition to his endorsement of active government measures to provide necessities for the improvement of the population, and to provide for the national defense, Hamilton lays tremendous emphasis on the concept of *national sovereign powers* in a way that echoes Vattel. One need only read Hamilton's *Defense of the Constitutionality of the National Bank* to grasp the importance of the sovereignty concept in his thought.

DEFENSE OF THE NATIONAL BANK

A brief summary of Hamilton's *tour de force* defending the constitutionality of establishing the National Bank

---

[9] I.e., that of David Hume; McDonald, *ibid.*, pp. 52-56.

will fill out the argument as to his uniquely American concept of this institution.

Hamilton wrote his *Opinion on the Constitutionality of the National Bank* for President George Washington, after Secretary of State Thomas Jefferson and Attorney General Edmund Randolph had vigorously opposed the Bank. They claimed that the Federal government did not have the Constitutional power to establish such a corporation, and urged President Washington to veto the bill, which had passed both Houses of Congress. (In fact, without the bank, power over the nation's finances would have been ceded to private foreign interests.) Hamilton's argument concentrated on the question of sovereignty: that the power of the government, "as to the objects intrusted to its management, is in its nature sovereign," and that the right of erecting corporations (in this case, the Bank of the United States, but the argument is more generally applicable) "is one, inherent in and inseparable from the idea of sovereign power."

Hamilton begins from the premise that "every power vested in a Government is in its nature *sovereign*, and includes by *force* of the *term*, a right to employ all the *means* requisite, and fairly *applicable* to the attainment of the *ends* of such power; and which are not precluded by restrictions and exceptions specified in the Constitution, or not immoral, or not contrary to the essential ends of political society." Those essential ends, of course, are laid out in the written Constitution, the which does not exist in the British kingdom.

After a lengthy exposition of how the Bank's role in aiding the collection of taxes, borrowing money, regulating trade, and providing for the common defense and general welfare will further the public good, Hamilton concludes that the chartering of the bank, with the government as a joint proprietor, will be a legitimate exercise of its sovereign power.

Countering Jefferson's and Randolph's narrow definition of the "necessary and proper" clause of the Constitution, Hamilton writes:

> This restrictive interpretation of the word *necessary* is also contrary to this sound maxim of construction namely, that the powers contained in a constitution of government, especially those which concern the general administration of the affairs of a country, its finances, trade, defence & *ought to be construed liberally, in advancement of the public good.*

> This rule does not depend on the particular form of a government or on the particular demarkation of the boundaries of its powers, but on the nature and objects of government itself. The means by which national exigencies are to be provided for, national inconveniencies obviated, national prosperity promoted, are of such infinite variety, extent and

complexity, that there must, of necessity, be great latitude of discretion in the selection & application of those means. Hence consequently, the necessity & propriety of exercising the authorities intrusted to a government on principles of liberal construction. [emphasis and paragraphing added]

Here we see Hamilton defending the Bank as part of the government's active direction of the national economy—not simply a support for the government's functioning, as in Great Britain. Later actions by the British government and its agents to destroy the U.S. national bank, especially the Second Bank of the United States, used the argument that its functioning oppressed smaller state banks, and provided too much credit by demeaning the role of specie. Such a "free trade" argument was bogus. It has been exhaustively documented that eliminating the Second National Bank only aided Wall Street's (and through Wall Street, London's) dominance of the U.S. financial system.[10]

---

[10] Bray Hammond, *ibid., passim.*

Japan and Germany both were inspired by the American System to industrialize their economics. Here you see Fukuzawa Yukichi, a leader of Japan's Meiji Restoration, and devotee of the American System, and

Otto von Bismarck, the German Chancellor who launched Germany's industrialization with American System methods. (stock.adobe.com)

CHAPTER 9

Hamilton's economics threatened to bring down the British Empire.

It has been frequently remarked that it seems to have been reserved to the people of this country, by their conduct and example, to decide the important question, whether societies of men are really capable or not of establishing good government from reflection and choice, or whether they are forever destined to depend for their political constitutions on accident and force.

–Alexander Hamilton, *Federalist* no. 1

AS HAMILTON MADE clear from the outset in the *Federalist Papers*, all eyes globally were on the American Republic in the period after its 1783 victory against the British Empire. The British Crown, as well as autocrats who shared its views, was exceedingly hopeful that the

"American experiment" would fail and was doing its best to ensure that it would, with measures ranging from economic warfare to funding popular revolts and Indian attacks. On the other hand, many leaders of the masses who were suffering under British imperialism elsewhere were watching eagerly in hopes of American success. After all, the American Revolution had been an international affair, in which republicans dedicated to liberty and progress from all around the world had flocked to join the Continental Army. They took the ideas they imbibed in America back home with them and tried to put them into effect.

While recognizing the significance of American success for the world strategic situation, President Washington and Treasury Secretary Hamilton were primarily focused on pulling the Union together in a lasting form around the new Constitution. But the reality of the debt crisis they faced, the desire and need for trade, and the danger of new armed conflicts with its neighbors, meant that they could not ignore foreign affairs. The United States in the 1790s had a broad swath of diplomatic relations,[1] with ambassadors or consulates in Algeria, the Austrian Empire, Denmark, France, Great Britain, various Italian city-states, Morocco, the Netherlands, the Papal states, Portugal, and Spain. President Washington also sent an ambassador to India (Calcutta) in 1792, then under the control of the British East India Company, although the Company

---

[1] Wikipedia, "History of United States Diplomatic Relations by Country."

never recognized him officially. Diplomatic relations with Prussia began in 1797, and with Russia in 1808, although there had been a consulate there since 1780.

Add to these official channels the voluminous correspondence which many of the Founding Fathers carried out with business partners, scientific collaborators, and former contributors to the American war with Britain, and there was an enormous potential conveyor belt for the ideas of Hamilton's American System to the four corners of the Earth.

From Alexander Hamilton's correspondence, for example, it can be documented that the *Report on Manufactures*, which had been published at least in part in New York newspapers (as well as Mathew Carey's *American Museum*), was republished in 1,000 copies in Dublin, Ireland in April of 1792 by Thomas Digges, who was in Ireland attempting to recruit workers for the Society for Useful Manufactures. In that same month Gouverneur Morris wrote to Hamilton that he needed a copy of Hamilton's economic reports to send to the Commerce Minister of Russia, Count Vorontsov, upon the request from his brother, who was the Russian ambassador to Great Britain.

In this chapter, I will trace some of the most significant results of the international conveyor belt of American System ideas, concentrating on those nations where national leaders adopted Hamiltonian economics, as they moved to throw off the yoke of British imperialism. While much is not known, Hamilton's influence—heavily through the mediation of Friedrich List and Henry Carey—is explicitly evident in Germany, Russia, Japan, and the early Chinese republic.[2] As these nations began to adopt Hamiltonian policies, especially in the latter part of the 19th Century, they represented a major threat to the British Empire.

THE CASE OF GERMANY

The influence of Hamiltonian economic thinking on the industrial development of Germany in the 19th Century is an open-and-shut case. The key American System conduits into that nation were Friedrich List and Henry C. Carey.

Friedrich List came to the United States in 1825, at the invitation of the Marquis de Lafayette. His activities as a professor of political economy in Germany had included working with an association of industrialists whose intent was to bring the various German principalities together into one German state. The purpose of this project was to facilitate industrialization and independence from the domination of the British Empire, as List had previously called for in proposing government credits for industry during his term in the Würtemberg parliament. This perspective had

---

[2] Sun Yat-sen, founder of the Chinese Republic, credited Abraham Lincoln's Gettysburg address as an inspiration for his three principles of the people. See Lyn Sharman, *Sun Yat-sen, his Life and its meaning, a critical biography*, Stanford, Stanford University Press, 1968.

aroused the ire of pro-British forces, and led him to be imprisoned, and finally exiled.[3]

In the United States, List worked in Pennsylvania in close collaboration with American System leaders around Mathew Carey, and began intensive study of the economic theories and policies underlying the then-rapid industrial development of the United States (under President John Quincy Adams). In 1827, he published the *Outlines of American Political Economy*, an attack on the British free-trade system and Adam Smith, which was financed by Carey's Society for the Promotion of Manufacturing and Mechanical Arts. His work, and that of Carey's son Henry, were to circulate throughout the world outside the British Empire—until the British succeeded in suppressing this knowledge, especially in the United States. In addition to publishing, List became intimately involved with the development of the railroad network in Pennsylvania, which was growing in tandem with the burgeoning coal industry.

List returned to Germany in the 1830s, where he resumed his work toward German reunification through industrialization. On Jan. 1, 1834, his program was largely realized, when Prussia joined with other German states in the Zollverein, or Customs Union; 18 states were soon united, within an external tariff barrier protecting them from British dumping. That same year,

---

[3] This section on List's history is described by Michael Liebig, "Friedrich List and the `American System' of Economy," in *Friedrich List, Outlines of American Political Economy, ibid.*, pp. 155-171.

List, now U.S. consul in Leipzig, proposed a Leipzig-Dresden railroad to begin a German national railway grid. Under the sponsorship of the king of Saxony, a railway company was formed, and the line was completed by 1837. Throughout this period List's influence grew, with backing from Alexander von Humboldt and his colleagues in the Prussian government. List's railroad magazine (*The Railroad Journal, or National Magazine of Inventions, Discoveries & Progress in Commerce, Industry, Public Undertakings & Public Institutions, and of Statistics of National Economy and Finance*) was particularly well received.

List's work came up against the sledgehammer of imperial opposition, but the ideas did not die. His ideas, and those of Henry Carey, who had also travelled in Europe during this period, merely remained dormant until the right international conditions were created by the American Civil War. Throughout that war, Carey's nationalist works were being translated into German, and distributed among leading and politically active circles in Germany. Among the converts was industrialist Wilhelm von Kardorff, who helped spread Carey's works on American political economy, and ultimately succeeded in convincing Chancellor Otto von Bismarck of the need to break with British free trade and industrialize.

Beginning in 1878, Bismarck initiated a top-down change in policy toward protection and government support for industrialization. A protective tariff for iron and steel manufacturers was adopted, along with a policy of state sponsorship of education and infrastructure development, including canals, railways, ports, merchant ships, and a modern navy. The shift led to the electrification of industry, and a huge leap in productivity. Suddenly, Germany moved into becoming the world's second-most powerful industrialized nation, after the United States. The "mighty" British empire was relegated to number three—due to the German adoption of American System methods.[4]

THE CASE OF RUSSIA

A Russian edition of Hamilton's 1791 *Report on the Usefulness of the Manufactories in Relation to Trade and Agriculture* was published in St. Petersburg, Russia in 1807. Minister of Finance D.A. Guryev sponsored the pamphlet. In an introduction, Russian educator V. Malinovsky wrote, "The similarity of American United Provinces with Russia appears both in the expanse of the land, climate and natural conditions, in the size of population disproportionate to the space, and in the general youthfulness of various generally useful institutions; therefore all the rules, remarks and means proposed here are suitable for our country."[5]

---

[4] Carey's influence in Germany is documented in depth by Anton Chaitkin in "How Carey and Bismarck Transformed Germany," *Executive Intelligence Review*, April 28, 2006.

[5] A full review of American System influence in 19th-Century Russia can be found in Rachel Douglas and Barbara Frazier,

Malinovsky and Guryev belonged to a faction of Russian scientists and statesmen who cherished the legacy of the programs Gottfried Leibniz drafted for Czar Peter the Great in the early 18th Century. The Russian Academy of Sciences was founded according to Leibniz's design, and, while it had been subjected to many assaults and subversions of its scientific and nation-building agenda by British- and Venetian-linked political and science figures, it remained a center of Leibnizian endeavor. Members of the Academy corresponded with America on scientific research, and closely watched the creation of the American republic. An Academy member, Franz Epinus, drafted the Treaty of Armed Neutrality, under which Russia and other continental European powers protected shipping against British attack during the American War of Independence.

Despite positive relations between Russia and the United States, shown in the close friendship of U.S. Ambassador John Quincy Adams with Czar Alexander I and his Chancellor Rumyantsev, American aid in building Russian railways,[6] and Russian support for the U.S. in the Civil War, oligarchical control kept the country in financial thrall to London. Russia kept a stiff protective

---

"The Fight to Bring the American System to 19th Century Russia", *Executive Intelligence Review*, January 3, 1992.

[6] For an exciting discussion of American involvement with Russia around its economic development, see Anton Chaitkin, "How Leibniz and Gauss Shaped America's Scientific Successes," *Executive Intelligence Review*, February 9, 1996.

tariff between 1825 and 1855, but, without a top-down commitment to industrial and agricultural reform, it could not develop. The substantial shift began with the 1860s alliance between Czar Alexander II and President Lincoln, and Alexander's abolition of serfdom. In the decades that followed, a small but powerful faction in the Russian Ministry of Finance and among the country's entrepreneurs fought to copy the American System against bitter opposition from the Russian landed nobility, who were backed by British and other international financiers.

The leading figures promoting the rapid industrialization process that took off in Russia were Dmitri Mendeleyev and Sergei Witte. The chemist Mendeleyev, under the influence of the German chemist Justus Liebig, founded Russian agro-chemistry, setting up experimental field stations in Russia's five soil-type regions, and beginning investigations into the effects of mineral fertilizers. Mendeleyev represented Russia at the 1867 International Paris Exposition, where he was able to make contact with Western industrialists and study the technologies presented, for possible introduction into Russia. Mendeleyev then toured every major chemical plant in Germany, France, and Belgium. When he returned, the government issued his findings as a book, *The Current Development of Certain Chemical Industries in Application to Russia–The World Exposition of 1867.*[7]

In 1868, Mendeleyev founded the Russian Chemical Society, to serve as a forum for scientific thought directed

[7] "Scientist, Statesman Fought British `Free Trade' in Russia," *Executive Intelligence Review,* Jan. 3, 1992.

to "building up the wealth of the country." Among this core group of scientists, industrialists, government officials, and financiers was Ivan A. Vyshnegradsky, a mechanical engineer, military technology expert, director of the Southwestern Railroad Company, and director of the St. Petersburg Technological Institute. Vyshnegradsky became Minister of Finance in 1889. His two most important accomplishments in office were the startup of the Trans-Siberian Railroad project and the drafting of a protective tariff. Among the men brought into his ministry to oversee these tasks were Mendeleyev, to chair the commission on the protective tariff, and Count Sergei Witte, then executive director of the Southwestern Railway Company, to head the new railroad department of the Finance Ministry.

Russia's Trans-Siberian Railroad, part of which is shown here, was built with the aid of Americans, and with the American Transcontinental Railroad in mind. (stock.adobe.com)

For Mendeleyev, the tariff commission was a platform from which to organize for the American System, which he had experienced firsthand on his trip to the Philadelphia Centennial Exposition in 1876.

Witte took over the Ministry of Finance in 1892 as a confirmed supporter of Friedrich List. He had translated List's book *National System of Political Economy* into Russian, which he thought provided the "solution for Russia." He envisioned a national rail infrastructure and increasing urbanization as key to his success, and began to organize Russia's finances accordingly.

Under his leadership, Russia began to take off economically. Railway development is exemplary: The 5,400-mile Trans-Siberian Railroad was completed on schedule in 1903; the amount of track laid from St. Petersburg to the Crimean Sea tripled. Railroads were the largest single industry in the country, employing 400,000 people in 1900, and were forcibly transforming other sectors. The metallurgical industries were developing apace, while approximately one-half of all finished metal products were railroad tracks. The oil and chemical industries were operating at full throttle, and coal production in the Donets Basin tripled between 1892 and 1903.

Under Witte's direction, government structure and financial policy were reorganized, in order, as he put it, to "give the country such industrial perfection as has been reached by the United States of America, which firmly bases its prosperity on two pillars—agriculture and industry." Russia's growth as an industrial power, including its outreach to collaboration with China, was an implicit threat to those British imperialists who sought to maintain control over the Eurasian "heartland."[8]

THE CASE OF JAPAN

The third country to explicitly adopt the Hamiltonian American System to overthrow feudalism and industrialize was Japan. The process took off in the 1860s, when a handful of Japanese intellectuals travelled to the United States, Germany, and Europe, and brought back the writings of Hamilton, Friedrich List, and Henry Carey. Upon their return home, they carried out what is called the Meiji Restoration in 1868 and proceeded over the next 25 years to crush the warlords, create a Constitution and a parliament, build a national railroad, found modern universities, and more than quintuple industrial and agriculture output.[9]

One of the leaders of this movement was Fukuzawa Yukichi, who visited the United States in 1860 and 1867. Fukuzawa concentrated on the process of education, including recruiting American advisers and professors to staff the Keio University he founded in

[8] Among the few English-language sources on Witte's policy is Sidney Harcave's *Count Sergei Witte and the Twilight of Imperial Russia*, Armonk, N.Y.: M.E. Sharpe, 2004.

[9] This history is presented in "Hamilton's Ghost Haunts Washington from Tokyo," by Kathy Wolfe, *Executive Intelligence Review*, January 3, 1992.

1858. "America is our Father," Fukuzawa said, and he worked with others to ensure that the works of key American economists, especially Henry and Mathew Carey, were translated into Japanese and circulated.

Fukuzawa's collaborators took positions in the Meiji government, where they carried out the work of industrialization, informed by missions sent to the United States and Europe to investigate the conditions and policies which had brought about the industrial revolution. In 1873, Toshimichi Okubo[10] founded the first National Bank of Japan, using the precise Hamiltonian model of turning government debt into the capital for issuing credit for industry and agriculture. Okubo acted on the advice of U.S. State Department representative Erasmus Peshine Smith,[11] a student of Henry Carey, who had been sent to Japan by President Ulysses S. Grant as an official economic adviser to the government.

Simultaneously, Okubo used the Industrial Promotion Board which he had founded to initiate, fund, and direct the industrialization process. Between 1873 and 1882, corporations were created in the areas of strategic importance, including shipbuilding,

---

[10] Toshimichi Okubo was one of the three main leaders of the Meiji Restoration. During his tenures of as Finance Minister and Home Affairs minister, he played a major role in the modernization of Japan until he was assassinated in 1878.

[11] E. Peshine Smith published his own attack on Malthusianism in 1853. He served as an adviser to the Japanese government from 1871-1876.

construction, cement, fertilizer, salt works, and textile mills, among others. In addition, the government built a national railway system. While many of these industries were initially government-operated, the government sold them to the private sector as soon as they could withstand the competition from the world's dominant financial powers.

During Smith's time in Tokyo, he promoted Henry Carey's system of protective tariffs and industrial development, the American System which Carey explicitly counterposed to feudalism, de-industrialization, and free trade, in works such as his 1851 pamphlet *The Harmony of Interest*. "The Japanese statesmen appear to have a sound notion of the policy of encouraging the protection of native industry," Smith wrote. His *Notes on Political Economy Designed Chiefly for Japanese Readers* was published in the *Tokyo Times*, for general circulation.

CURTAINS FOR THE BRITISH EMPIRE?

Germany, Russia, and Japan were not the only nation states to imitate the American System, especially in the period after the U.S. Civil War. Government-directed industrialization policies directly or indirectly derived from U.S. Hamiltonians were also being adopted at that time in France under Prime Minister Gabriel Hanotaux; in Brazil under Finance Minister Ruy Barbosa; in Colombia under President Rafael Nuñez;

and elsewhere. But it was the potential combination of the industrial powerhouses of the United States, Germany, Russia, and Japan which threatened to break the control then being wielded by the 19th-Century global British Empire.

Historically, the British Empire had strong roots and factions within all four nations, especially through the royal courts. Intermarriages among the British, German, and Russian princely houses facilitated powerful influence for the British government, despite conflicts such as the Crimean War, where Russia and the British (among others) fought each other.[12] But the example of the extraordinary economic growth of the United States under Lincoln, and the outreach by U.S. industrialists and Republican administrations to contribute to the similar industrialization of other nations, had built up the basis for breaking that control. The ideals of the American Revolution, which had inspired the world a century before, had now shown themselves to be a viable proposition: in Lincoln's words, "the last best hope of Earth."

The affinity which Germany, Russia, and Japan, in particular, felt for the American cause was epitomized by the extraordinarily friendly welcome given to former President Ulysses S. Grant during his world tour in 1877-1879.

It is far beyond the scope of this book to review the political machinations by which the British Empire,

---

[12] It may surprise many to know that the United States sided with Russia in this conflict. One write-up can be found here.

led by King Edward VII, succeeded in breaking up the alliances which could have sealed its doom. Suffice it to say that the Russo-Japanese War, and the rising conflict between Germany and Russia which followed the dismissal of Chancellor Bismarck, can be traced to British skullduggery, as can the interruption of Russian Chancellor Witte's industrialization program by the 1905 Revolution. Within the United States, a similar destructive shift occurred with the ascendance to the Presidency of Theodore Roosevelt, who moved to break friendly U.S. relations with Germany and Russia, in particular, and establish (long before Winston Churchill) the "special relationship" with the Empire of Great Britain.

With the dawn of the 20th Century came the virtual interment of the American System as a political-economic concept. Thus, the actual source of the nation's extraordinary progress was increasingly erased from political and academic dialogue, in favor of the idea of the Smithian free enterprise, *laissez faire* concept. This occurred at the same time that Wall Street financiers such as the House of Morgan succeeded in taking over large swaths of U.S. industry, which they had not created, but could use to their advantage.[13] And

---

[13] In a letter to his father dated April 29, 1874, J.P. Morgan wrote, "I have come to the conclusion that neither my firm nor myself will have anything to do, hereafter, directly or indirectly, with the negotiation of securities of any undertaking not entirely completed. . ." (quoted in Ron Chernow, *The House of Morgan* [1990], p. 37).

despite the extraordinary success of President Franklin Roosevelt in implementing Hamiltonian policies to revive the nation from the Wall Street-provoked Great Depression, the ideology of radical free-market economics has regained hegemony, not only in the United States, but in much of the Western world. The disastrous results of this process are writ large in our increasing death rates, opioid epidemic, decrepit railways, and collapsing bridges—not to mention the stagnating level of Total Factor Productivity in the economy as a whole.

One critical step toward reversing this decay must be to revive an understanding of the principles of Hamilton's American System.

An etching showing the Constitutional Convention of 1787 being addressed by George Washington.

CHAPTER 10

Hamilton's political economy is key to saving our Constitutional republic

Mutual wants constitute one of the strongest links of political connection, and the extent of these bears a natural proportion to the diversity in the means of mutual supply. Suggestions of an opposite complexion are ever to be deplored, as unfriendly to the steady pursuit of one great common cause, and to the perfect harmony of all the parts.

—*Report on Manufactures*

WITHOUT ALEXANDER HAMILTON'S efforts and ideas, the current Constitution of the United States would not have been adopted, and perhaps there would be no United States at all. And now that Hamilton's American System of economics has been virtually erased from popular memory, there is a real danger that our government will either collapse or cease to be a republic. For without the commitment to economic progress which drove the adoption of the Constitution, and which it embodies, there is a dwindling basis for our nation to survive.

There have been many periods of crisis such as we experience today, where Americans were at each other's throats. Even the process of ratification of the Constitution was extremely contentious. The major states of Virginia and New York almost didn't ratify. In the view of some, only the threat of New York City seceding from the state pushed the New York State anti-Federalists into finally approving the document.[1] Secessions by the Northeastern states from the Union were threatened periodically during the 1800s[2] and 1810s.[3] Then, of course, there was the Civil War, whose wounds have never been thoroughly healed, despite the considerable efforts of the Franklin Roosevelt

---

[1] Pauline Maier, *Ratification: The People Debate the Constitution, 1787-1788* (New York: Simon and Schuster, 2010), 343, 381. Without New York's ratification, there could have been no continental republic.

[2] A plot to have New York State join the New England states in seceding was suspected by Hamilton in 1804 and was part of his motivation to stop Aaron Burr's campaign for governor. There are numerous Hamilton letters to New England Federalists imploring them not to destroy the Constitution.

[3] I refer to the infamous Hartford Convention of 1814–1815 which occurred during Federalist agitation for Northern secession. Respected historian Samuel Eliot Morrison, however, argues that the Federalists never really intended to break up the Union.

Administration, in particular. Perhaps the period of the greatest sense of unity, as well as of physical progress, came during the World War II mobilization, which held the promise—once the Nazis were defeated—of bringing about a great peacetime renaissance of harmony and scientific progress.

Why has the "more perfect Union" not been achieved? Because there has been a constant attack on the American System which Hamilton envisioned, coming not only from the British oligarchy *per se*, but from financial interests who have shared their degraded view of man and society, and have dominated the political agenda. These interests have succeeded to an alarming extent in subverting the U.S. (and world) financial system into a machine that grinds up populations in the name of economic nostrums, demands de-industrialization and even depopulation, and creates the scarcities and jealousies that turn neighbor against neighbor, nation state against nation state. China's recent phenomenal economic growth and reduction of poverty have been rare exceptions to this global trend.

This global situation calls out for a resurrection of Hamilton's American System principles, leading to a resolution of the unresolved conflict within the United States itself. But let's first review some relevant history.

A "More Perfect Union"

> We the People of the United States, in Order to form a more perfect Union, establish Justice, ensure domestic Tranquility, provide for the common defense, promote the general Welfare, and secure the Blessings of Liberty for ourselves and our posterity, do ordain and establish this Constitution for the United States of America.

That Preamble was not just a felicitous turn of phrase to those Founding Fathers who fought to bring about the establishment of our Constitutional republic. The goals which it set out for the nation defined its very purpose, and the elaboration of the powers of the various departments of our government which followed was intended to outline the means to those ends. The Preamble called for "a more perfect union" and "domestic tranquility" because the confederation of sovereign colonies was literally disintegrating in (British-aided) internecine warfare. Unable to pay its veterans or its debt, torn apart by trade war, and under virtual embargo by Great Britain, the victorious Confederation was on the verge of collapse.[4]

---

[4] See John Fiske, *The Critical Period of American History, 1783-1789*, Houghton Mifflin Company, Boston and New York, 1888, *passim*.

One major source of conflict was competition between the states, with port states like New York taxing those without shipping outlets, and small states chafing under the dominance of the larger ones. Another was the longer-standing conflict between the countryside and the cities. The young Alexander Hamilton had addressed this division back in his 1775 *Farmer Refuted*, where he argued against the Tory Samuel Seabury's assertion that the non-importation agreement adopted by the First Continental Congress was a move by the urban population and the merchants against the interests of the farmers. The prosperity of both farmer and merchant was interdependent, Hamilton argued, as each provided the outlet for the other's goods, and fulfilled their consumer demands. The British attempt to foment political division between farmer and city-dweller was merely a means of maintaining British control.

During the Revolutionary conflict itself, these divides had been muted. But if the nation was to avoid disintegration, they would have to be addressed.

The Constitution called for the promotion of the General Welfare not only in the Preamble, but also in Article I, Section 8, as if to underline the importance of Federal government action to improve conditions of life for all the people. And, uniquely among world constitutions, the Preamble calls for the securing of the blessings of liberty not only for the current population of the country, but also for "posterity"—thus demanding that the Federal government provide for the future in the actions it takes today.

In other words, contrary to the all-too-common view that the Constitution was meant to protect the American population from a tyrannical Federal authority, the Constitution was actually established to *create* a Federal authority with the power to protect and advance the population. Without a central authority with the ability to fulfill the commitment laid out in the Preamble, the nation was in mortal danger.

President George Washington and Treasury Secretary Alexander Hamilton were among the Founding Fathers most committed to this perspective. Even while the Revolutionary War was still raging, both began to concern themselves with the need to set up national institutions which could deal with the economic devastation being caused not only by the war, but also by the social and sectional rivalries which often threatened to paralyze the war effort.[5] One key vehicle for creating a stable foundation for the nation, Hamilton asserted, was a National Bank and banking system that could provide credit for the sustenance and advancement of the nation's people.[6] But, to have a

---

[5] Hamilton's correspondence, beginning with his letter to Continental Congressman James Duane in 1779, is rife with discussion of how to deal with looming economic disaster. His exchanges with Washington reflect their agreement on the need for creating a central government that could deal with the economy.

[6] See Hamilton's famous letter of April 30, 1781 to incoming Superintended of Finance Robert Morris, where he

national bank, one first needed to have a Nation—not just a bunch of squabbling mini-states. The creation of the Constitution, which Hamilton probably did more than any other single individual to bring into existence,[7] was absolutely essential.

Not all the participants in the Constitutional Convention agreed with Hamilton's positive nationalist perspective.[8] Many delegates continued to assert their allegiance to their states rather than to the nation as a whole. But the vast majority was unwilling to let the Convention fail and the process of disintegration proceed. Many participants even saw the framing of this document as an enterprise of world-historical significance.

As Hamilton put it in the first *Federalist* paper: "It has been frequently remarked that it seems to have been reserved to the people of this country, by their conduct and example, to decide the important question, whether societies of men are really capable or not of establishing good government from reflection and choice, or whether they are forever destined to depend

---

emphasizes that the main problem facing the country is "introducing order into our finances—it is by restoring public credit—not by gaining battles, that we are finally to gain our object."

[7] Hamilton's key role in drafting the call for the Constitutional Convention at the end of the "failed" Annapolis Convention of 1786, and in fighting for ratification are cases in point.

[8] Hamilton's view was shared by a core of delegates which included Washington, Gouverneur Morris, James Wilson, Benjamin Franklin, and, at that point, James Madison.

for their political constitutions on accident and force."
Gouverneur Morris, the Hamilton ally who, as a
member of the Committee on Style, produced the final
draft of the document, is reported to have commented
that he came to the Constitutional Convention not
as a representative of his state (he was a delegate from
Pennsylvania), but "as a representative of America,—a
representative in some degree of the whole human race,
for the whole human race would be affected by the
outcome of the convention."[9]

A FUNCTIONING ECONOMY

"A unity of commercial, as well as political, interests
can only result from a unity of government," argued
Alexander Hamilton in *Federalist* No. 11. He identified
the way in which the strong points of the economy in
the various states complemented each other and would
contribute to the greater prosperity of the nation as a
whole. Once a unified government was created, he
said, the United States could escape the dominion of
the European powers. He concluded this essay with the
rallying cry:

> Let Americans disdain to be the
> instruments of European greatness! Let
> the thirteen States, bound together in

[9] Arnold Whitridge, "A Representative of America," *American Heritage*, vol. 27, issue 4, June 1976.

a strict and indissoluble Union, concur
in erecting one great *American system*
superior to the control of all transatlantic
force of influence and able to dictate the
terms of the connection between the old
and the new world! [emphasis added]

The fact that the people of the United States,
through special conventions, ratified the Constitution
did not mean that they necessarily agreed with
Hamilton's perspective, however. Indeed, the issue
of whether the Constitution established the power of
the Federal government to take action to promote the
general welfare through economic measures came to a
head almost immediately.

Opposition became particularly intense with
Hamilton's proposal for Federal assumption of the war
debts, and the establishment of the Bank of the United
States. The primary purpose of that bank, the Treasury
Secretary stressed, was to use the Federal debt as the
means of establishing a financial corporation that would
issue credit into the economy, and thus expand industry,
commerce, and agriculture—i.e. create prosperity for
the nation as a whole. It would also create a national
currency, facilitate the collection of taxes, and provide
aid to the Federal government when necessary.

Secretary of State Thomas Jefferson and his allies
(led by House Speaker Madison and Attorney General
Edmund Randolph) objected. They claimed that the
Federal government could not establish a corporation,

because the Constitution didn't explicitly say it could, and that the government could function without it. Behind their objections, was the fear that the creation of the Bank would increase the power of the Federal government (including to eliminate slavery)—and they wanted more power to remain with the state governments. Jefferson had been lukewarm, or worse,[10] in supporting the Constitution to begin with. To the extent he understood Washington's and Hamilton's conception of the economic development of the country, he virulently disagreed.[11]

As I reviewed in Chapter 8, Hamilton won President Washington's support for the Bank against Jefferson, and the Bank of the United States came into being. Jefferson's response was to launch a newspaper war against Hamilton, effectively beginning the two-party system. But for 20 years the Bank played an important role in securing the nation (although much less so under Jefferson's Secretary of the Treasury Albert Gallatin). Yet the criticisms by the Jeffersonian party continued, including with the argument that the Bank

---

[10] Hamilton charged that Jefferson actually opposed the ratification of the Constitution in two 1792 series of essays, *An American*, and *Catullus*.

[11] Jefferson opposed banks, urbanization, and often manufactures per se. In 1800 he wrote: "I view great cities as pestilential to the morals, the health and the liberties of man. True, they nourish some of the elegant arts; but the useful ones can thrive elsewhere; and less perfection in the others, with more health, virtue and freedom, would be my choice."

was favoring the manufacturing and commercial states, to the detriment of the South and the West.

Hamilton took on this argument in *The Report on Manufactures*, insisting that the Bank's credit system was crucial for national unity and prosperity. "The *aggregate* prosperity of manufactures, and the *aggregate* prosperity of Agriculture are intimately connected," he wrote. [emphasis in the original] "Perhaps the superior steadiness of the demand of a domestic market for the surplus produce of the soil, is alone a convincing argument of its truth."

"Mutual wants constitute one of the strongest links of political connection, and the extent of these bears a natural proportion to the diversity in the means of mutual supply," he continued. "Suggestions of an opposite complexion are ever to be deplored, as unfriendly to the steady pursuit of one great common cause, and to the perfect harmony of all the parts."

These arguments unfortunately did not carry the day, as shown in the defeat of the BUS's re-charter in 1811, and the ensuing disastrous effects during the War of 1812.

STARKE'S LOUISIANA BRIGADE FIGHTING WITH STONES AT THE EMBANKMENT NEAR THE "DEEP CUT."

Confederates and Unionists fight hand-to-hand at Deep Cut, Virginia.

"Free trade" caused the Civil War

The revival of Hamilton's credit policy in the Biddle-run Second Bank of the United States led to considerable progress in bringing the Union together in the 1820s. Following the landmark Steamboat (*Gibbons vs. Ogden*) case decision[12] by Supreme Court Chief Justice John Marshall in 1824, President Monroe

---

[12] For a discussion of this case and its relation to Hamilton's American System, see "Steamboat Case Clears the Way for the American System" by Edward Spannaus, printed on https://americansystemnow. It can be accessed here.

acknowledged the Federal government's constitutional authority to fund infrastructure. The passage of the General Survey Act that year allocated funds for the Army Corps of Engineers to begin planning work for the country's transportation network.

Canals and railroads began to crisscross the country, bringing prosperity to the less-populated western lands. Farmers were able to access credit and sell their goods, while merchants and manufacturers obtained their necessary supplies, and saw their markets grow. Under these circumstances, mechanization of agriculture began to spread, and the inefficiency of slave labor became more and more obvious.

Writing in 1853, in his study of *The Slave Trade Domestic and Foreign*, American System economist Henry Carey characterized the development of the economy in the period from 1824 to 1833, as exposing the inefficiency of slave labor, and putting it on the path to extinction. "… [M]ills and furnaces increased in number, and there was a steady increase in the tendency toward the establishment of local places of exchange; and then it was that Virginia held her convention at which was last discussed in that State the question of emancipation." The convention ended in a stalemate.

Carey argued that the policies of the Jackson Administration in its second term—namely, the repeal of high tariffs, and the withdrawal of Federal deposits from the Second Bank of the United States—led to the ensuing strengthening of the pro-slavery forces. He wrote:

In 1833, however, protection was abandoned, and a tariff was established by which it was provided that we should, in a few years, have a system of merely revenue duties; and from that date the abandonment of the older State proceeded with a rapidity never before known, and with it grew the domestic slave trade and the pro-slavery feeling. Then it was that were passed the laws restricting emancipation and prohibiting education; and then it was that the exports of slaves from Virginia and the Carolinas was so great that the population of those States remained almost, if not quite stationary, and the growth of the black population fell from thirty percent, in the ten previous years, to twenty-four percent. ...[13]

Carey insisted that the expansion of slavery was "the natural consequence of our submission, even in part, to the system that looks to compelling the export of raw products, the exhaustion of the land, the cheapening of labour, and the export of the labourer. Wherever it is resisted, slavery dies away and freedom grows."

---

[13] These excerpts from *The Slave Trade Domestic and Foreign*, as well as those above and below, come from the website American History, from Revolution to Reconstruction. They can be found here.

The system Carey attacked was the result of the abandonment of Hamiltonian policies of government support for manufactures and infrastructure. In an open letter to Congressman Henry Wilson in 1867, Carey was explicit: "Slavery *did not* make the rebellion [the Civil War—ed.]... British free trade gave us sectionalism, and promoted the growth of slavery, and thus led to the rebellion."[14] (emphasis in original) As a result of that free trade policy, large parts of the country were cut off from industrial and infrastructure development. In an open letter to Ulysses Grant, in the wake of Grant's victory in the 1868 Presidential election. Carey noted how the Federal government's policy of *laissez faire* had left huge swaths of the country without development and without infrastructure such as railroads. The rail system, he noted, is totally sectional, with virtually no North-South connections. He wrote:

> *Had our policy been different—had we strengthened the center—there would have been such a growth of domestic commerce that roads would have been made running north and south, northeast and southwest southeast and northwest, thereby so tying together the various parts of the Union as to render it wholly impossible that the idea of secession should continue to have existence.* [emphasis added]

---

[14] Reprinted in W. Allen Salisbury, *The Civil War and the American System, America's Battle with Britain, 1860-1876,* second edition, *EIR*, Washington, D.C., 1992.

President Lincoln, despite the war, had aggressively pursued policies to bind the nation together, most notably with the Transcontinental Railroad. And he knew that the only way to heal the nation's wounds following the war was with economic progress permeating every corner of the nation. But despite good intentions on the part of Republican presidents such as Ulysses S. Grant, the British financial power and its junior partners in Wall Street were able to prevent that from happening. Tariffs were reduced, greenbacks were cut back, and the Southern oligarchical plantation system was allowed to revive, leaving the freed slaves in a condition of virtual serfdom. Instead of nationwide economic integration, the country became increasingly split between an industrialized North, and a rural impoverished South, thus maintaining the fault lines which we continue to be plagued by today.

THE CONSTITUTION DEMANDS ECONOMIC PROGRESS

After a long hiatus, the presidency of Franklin Roosevelt launched a revival of a policy to strengthen the Union by building up the economy in every part of the country. FDR's New Deal programs deliberately aimed to leave no area untouched. Huge sections of the nation, such as the seven-state Tennessee Valley and the Southwest, underwent a dramatic transformation. The Tennessee River watershed went from a malaria-infested, impoverished backwater to a home for modern agriculture and industry, thanks to FDR's Tennessee Valley Authority. Rural electrification, by going against the demands by the private power companies, turned on the lights in parts of the country that had been neglected because they were considered unprofitable. By eliminating the isolation of many parts of the country, FDR increased the potential for national unity and prosperity.

A similar process of unification occurred during the war mobilization, during which areas of the Southwest and West became industrial hubs for the first time. Cities like Seattle, Portland (Oregon), San Francisco, Los Angeles, and San Diego became thriving, if overcrowded, metropolises, and the living standards of millions of Americans were raised.

Since FDR's death, the United States has increasingly turned its back on the requirement that the Federal government take positive action to implement the full panoply of commitments set out in Preamble of our Constitution. Hamilton's arguments for Constitutional action on behalf of the general welfare have been all but buried in the fraudulent assertions that "the government isn't the solution; it's the problem." President Franklin Roosevelt had correctly stressed the complete opposite: that a weak government simply meant the ceding of power to "private autocratic powers," and the consequent immiseration of, and disunity among, the people.

FDR put it this way in his acceptance <u>speech</u> before the 1936 Democratic Party Convention:

> For too many of us the political equality we once had won was meaningless in the face of economic inequality. A small group had concentrated into their own hands an almost complete control over other people's property, other people's money, other people's labor—other people's lives. For too many of us life was no longer free; liberty no longer real; men could no longer follow the pursuit of happiness.
>
> Against economic tyranny such as this, the American citizen could appeal only to the organized power of Government. The collapse of 1929 showed up the despotism for what it was. The election of 1932 was the people's mandate to end it. Under that mandate it is being ended.
>
> The royalists of the economic order have conceded that political freedom was the business of the Government, but they have maintained that economic slavery was nobody's business. They granted that the Government could protect the citizen in his right to vote, but they

denied that the Government could do anything to protect the citizen in his right to work and his right to live.

Today we stand committed to the proposition that freedom is no half-and-half affair. If the average citizen is guaranteed equal opportunity in the polling place, he must have equal opportunity in the market place.

These economic royalists complain that we seek to overthrow the institutions of America. What they really complain of is that we seek to take away their power. Our allegiance to American institutions requires the overthrow of this kind of power. In vain they seek to hide behind the Flag and the Constitution. In their blindness they forget what the Flag and the Constitution stand for. Now, as always, they stand for democracy, not tyranny; for freedom, not subjection; and against a dictatorship by mob rule and the over-privileged alike.

Does not the disunity and income inequality we see today resonate with these crises of the past? Huge regions of the country lack the sophisticated (although pathetically outdated) infrastructure available to residents of the East and West Coasts. Rural regions suffer disproportionately in terms of lack of jobs, vital resources (like hospitals), and income, with a resulting massive disparity of "diseases of despair"[15] in those areas. The electoral map[16] in the last Presidential election dramatizes the point: Our failure to follow a Hamiltonian economic policy has split the nation in ways that portend disaster.

Perhaps it is only in times of crisis—such as the United States faced in FDR's time, as in the period in which the Constitution was founded–that our citizenry (and Congress) will discover the positive unifying role which our Federal government was crafted by Alexander Hamilton and his allies to play. One would hope that such a realization, and the consequent implementation of American System economic policies, would occur before the nation faces an even larger catastrophe than that we suffer today.

---

[15] See Ann Case and Angus Deaton, "Mortality and Morbidity in the 21st Century," Brookings Institution, August 2107. For the article, click here.

[16] See a map here. It shows the nation split between the Coasts and the vast mid-section, evoking the old urban/rural split.

Rapid expansion of nuclear fission power, on the way to developing nuclear fusion, would dramatically improve U.S. productivity.

CHAPTER 11

A Hamiltonian Vision for Today

As a general marches at the head of troops, so ought wise politicians, if I dare use the expression, to march at the head of affairs; insomuch that they ought not to await the event, to know what measures to take, but the measures which they have taken ought to produce the event.

–Demosthenes,[1] as quoted in Hamilton's 1776–77 paybook

LETTING WALL STREET and its banking practices dominate our nation's economic policy has led us to the brink of disaster. Our Total Factor Productivity is

---

[1] Demosthenes was a statesman in 4th Century BC Athens who was renowned for his oratory. His speeches rallying Athenians against Philip of Macedon led to the coinage of the phrase Philippics to refer to inflammatory speeches.

in the basement, our infrastructure is antiquated and collapsing, and the United States is now alone among advanced nations in having a declining life expectancy. The nation lacks the unity of purpose to deal with its crises and move ahead. We are in desperate need of applying the principles of Alexander Hamilton's American System.

The preceding chapters have elaborated those principles. They can be summarized as follows:

- National sovereign control over the nation's currency.
- Establishment of a source of Federal government-backed credit for spurring scientific and technological breakthroughs, including in major infrastructure projects, to ensure economic growth and prosperity.
- Promotion and protection of the productive powers of labor through Federal government oversight and programs (cf. health insurance, pensions)—the general welfare.
- Federal leadership to create "a more perfect Union" through setting national goals that will advance the nation as a whole.

Each of the American System Presidents whom we have discussed applied these principles, bringing the nation to greater levels of productivity, power, and happiness. What would application of those principles look like today?

THE JFK CHALLENGE

One guideline emerges from examining the intentions of our last American System President, John F. Kennedy, intentions brutally cut off by his assassination. Kennedy's agenda for the nation in the 1960s remained mostly unfulfilled, and in many respects is still highly relevant for us today.

His grandest goal, of course, was the Apollo <u>Moon Project</u>,[2] which was gloriously achieved six years after his death. That landing on the Moon brought the United States economy its last major injection of technological innovation, bringing us lasers, micro-computers, and other "space-age" technologies which have revolutionized our world. The Apollo mission cost the Federal government $25 billion (in 1960s dollars) but <u>paid back</u> many times that in its impact on productivity. At the same time, the mobilization for the Moon landing raised the morale of the U.S. population, creating the basis for national unity and greater progress.

Yet, the full goals of Kennedy's space program were never fulfilled. Kennedy conceived of the Moon landing as a stepping stone to the broadest exploration of space, including human space flight to other locations, such as Mars. That program continues to be sabotaged through the kind of accountants' small-mindedness that Hamilton abhorred.

---

[2] For an overview of the project, see NASA's retrospective analysis.

President Kennedy had his eye on other technological frontiers as well, whose expression can be found in the speeches which he gave on his September 1963 "conservation" tour across the United States. One of those frontiers was the rapid expansion of nuclear energy, which he virtually <u>predicted</u> in his speech in Hanford, Washington would be providing the lion's share of electric power for the country by the end of the 20th Century.[3]

Another was the use of nuclear power to desalinate sea water, a proposal which Kennedy made in August 1962 at the opening of California's San Luis Dam, and then acted on by establishing a taskforce in January 1963 dedicated to exploring this issue. The taskforce, coordinated by the Executive Office of Science and Technology in cooperation with the Atomic Energy Commission and the Interior Department, proposed rapidly moving ahead with such a program. (Coincidentally, Hamilton, a member of the American Philosophical Society, wrote a letter to Thomas Jefferson in June 1792 in which he proposed distillation of seawater for use on U.S. ships.)

The third major area Kennedy identified as a scientific frontier involved water management. As he said in the 1962 Hanford speech cited above, not a drop of water should be wasted from the great rivers flowing through the nation into the sea. This kind of thinking led him to express interest in the work being done by Utah Senator Frank Moss, who was working

---

[3] This prediction was made by President Kennedy on Sept. 26, 1963 in a speech at the Hanford nuclear reactor site.

on the huge water management plan being developed by the Parsons Company, the North American Water and Power Alliance (<u>NAWAPA</u>). Sen. Moss went on to sponsor a Senate Resolution calling for NAWAPA to be studied by the International Joint Commission, a group comprised of Canadians and Americans. Among the cosponsors was Sen. Robert F. Kennedy.

All three of these areas championed by President Kennedy—space, nuclear power, and grand-scale water management—should actually be on the U.S. agenda today. But unless Hamiltonian principles are re-adopted, that cannot happen.

SOME CONCRETE PROPOSALS

FINANCE

The first task for a Hamiltonian revival would be the restoration of national control over the U.S. dollar. That would mean junking the current floating exchange-rate system, which has resulted in trillions of dollars being generated internationally for speculative purposes. Money should be tied to production.

The second would be to re-establish sanity in the U.S. banking system by the restoration of FDR's Glass-Steagall Act of 1933, which mandated separation of commercial from investment banking. Such a measure would eliminate *de facto* U.S. government support for Wall Street's speculative ventures, and should be accompanied by other anti-speculative measures, such as restoring the previous SEC ban on stock-buybacks. Banking should be regulated so as to encourage and reward investment in the physical economy.

The third would be to create a new source of long-term, low-interest credit in the form of a <u>National Infrastructure Bank</u>,[4] or a Third Bank of the United States. Such a bank, created on Hamiltonian principles, would use already existent government debt to capitalize an institution that would lend to, and partner with, state governments and companies on major infrastructure projects which this country so desperately needs. The scale should be large—at least $4 trillion, to start to meet not only current needs, but the needs of the future.

A magnetically levitated train in Shanghai, China. Maglev is the wave of the future in ground transport.

---

[4] See Appendix 2 for a current Hamiltonian proposal.

INFRASTRUCTURE

At the top of the list would be the financing of a *high-speed rail network* throughout the country, preferably using maglev technology.[5] This network should be electrified, thus requiring a quantum leap in electricity generation—a task for a rejuvenated nuclear industry. Supplementing long–distance rail should be electrified urban transit. All these projects, one might note, answer the current widespread concerns about traffic gridlock and auto pollution, real problems which are now being addressed by exorbitant tolls and various forms of intrusive social engineering.

Of equally crucial importance would be *upgrading of the national energy grid*, with the objective of a dramatic increase in electricity production with increasingly efficient fuels. These would emphasize nuclear fission energy, which is the most efficient form of electricity generation currently available, but now being shut down by financial markets rigged against it. Plans for fourth-generation, even safer nuclear plants are well advanced, and proposals for building small modular reactors (which could be done more cheaply and on an assembly line) are quite feasible. Just as Hamilton

---

[5] Maglev stands for magnetic levitation. Trains using maglev are suspended by a superconducting magnet above the track and therefore do not experience the friction of moving by rail. The idea for maglev trains was developed at Brookhaven labs in the U.S., but has only been put into practice in Japan, South Korea, and China.

designated iron as a crucial strategic industry for government support, so this most high-tech form of energy production should be designated as a strategic priority today.

This expansion should take place in the context of finally financing a crash program for nuclear fusion energy,[6] which was proposed and passed the Congress in 1980, but has never been funded! The bill was the McCormack Magnetic Fusion Engineering Act, and it committed the United States to building a prototype magnetic fusion reactor by the year 2000. President Carter signed it, and Congress has refused to fund it.

The third urgent area is water management, as demonstrated by the ongoing devastation from floods and droughts (and consequent forest fires) which have ravaged the country over recent years, and the highly dangerous state of the nation's water and sewer network (e.g., the contamination of decades-old drinking water pipes by lead and other dangerous substances, as in the infamous Flint, Michigan case). An updated desalination program, along with a new NAWAPA project, and the replacement of antiquated piping

---

[6] Nuclear fusion is a means of generating energy through fusing atoms, rather than splitting them as does fission. It can be fueled by isotopes from non-radioactive materials such as helium 3, hydrogen, and oxygen, thus dramatically decreasing its cost of fuel, and the danger of contamination. More information can be found from the World Nuclear Association.

throughout the country, are prime projects for a new infrastructure bank.

SCIENCE

In the concluding section of the *Report on Manufactures*, Hamilton made a plea for a federally-sponsored board to promote "the encouragement of new inventions and discoveries." While the United States nominally has several such institutions, the deindustrialization of the country and lack of a proper credit source have led either to the underfunding of worthwhile initiatives (such as research on cancer and fusion), or the wastage of funds on frivolous or destructive projects (such as studying–i.e., promoting– the use of mind-destroying drugs like marijuana).

A Hamiltonian approach to financing—prioritizing investment in the *physical* (versus money and service) economy and its productivity—will permit a real science offensive, in the tradition of FDR's Manhattan Project, or Kennedy's Apollo program.

Just as Hamilton's vision was to use his financial system to qualitatively transform a slave-based, agricultural economy beholden to England, into an independent, thriving industrial republic, so the application of Hamilton's principles today would create a qualitative transformation.

Nuclear fusion, for example, would represent a total revolution in the economy. It would vastly cheapen energy production and provide the means to transform junk materials into useful ones (the <u>fusion torch</u>).[7] No longer would human beings be consigned to digging in the dirt and scrambling frantically to eke out an existence. The environment would be cleaned; needed physical infrastructure connecting parts of our nation, and our nation with others, could be produced more efficiently than we now can even conceive; populations would be uplifted to living standards appropriate to fostering human creativity. Exploration of space would become a feasible prospect, providing new horizons for studying the universe and the phenomenon of life itself.

Such an economy would finally fulfill Hamilton's admonition for us to create an economic system which would "cherish and stimulate the human mind."

---

[7] The fusion torch is a proposed way of using the nuclear fusion plasma to separate metallic junk into its components, thereby allowing those component to be re-used.

GLOSSARY OF ECONOMIC TERMS

I HAVE PROVIDED these definitions of some of the economic terms used frequently in the text because they are either not in general use, or connote something other than what is generally understood today. Some of these terms need to have their meaning clarified in the context of Hamilton's economic thinking.

Bounties: Bounties are a category of reward, premium, or subsidy provided to an industry which a government wishes to encourage. They were used in the United States during the course of the 19th Century.

Economic Progress: Economic progress, as used in this book, never refers to increases in GDP or other such monetary measures, but rather to the increase in living standards of the population, the creation of more powerful and efficient forms of production, and the freeing of mankind to be able to increasingly use his mind and develop his human creative potential.

Infrastructure: Infrastructure is used in this book as synonymous with the early American concept of internal improvements, i.e. the creation of man-made systems of either a physical or cultural kind that structure national economic and cultural life. Infrastructure spans systems of transportation, communication, water use, housing, and power generation. It also concerns systems of education, health, science, and the arts.

Physical economy: I use this term to clarify that I am talking about the physical product and conditions of society, as distinct from the financial sphere. Physical economy does not concern itself with financial flows, or financial profits, but with the efficiency, quality, and output of manufacturing, agriculture, and physical infrastructure.

Political economy: Political economy, as distinct from economics as such, deals with the system of laws and government which organize economic processes within a nation. Thus a political economist would never analyze an economy by comparing it to a household (as Aristotle did), but would rather begin from the societal level, from which the nation's economic relationships are organized. Alexander Hamilton was a political economist, a nation-builder, organizing society to achieve certain economic (and other) ends, not an economist *per se*.

Productivity: Productivity generally refers to the amount of output that can be produced with a given input, either in labor, raw materials, or time. The preferred Hamiltonian term, however, is the *productive powers of labor*, which depends upon the quality of the machinery, the level of education or health of the workers, the quality of the inputs, and the state of the infrastructure on which the productive process depends. In other words, a factory which surpasses others in output, with the same number of workers, by virtually working them to death, is not actually more productive than its competitor which provides its workers with decent working conditions and modern machinery.

Technological progress: Technological progress is used in this book to refer to qualitative advances in the technologies used in basic industry and day-to-day life. Examples would be the replacement of wood burning for fuel by fossil fuels, or the use of the internal combustion engine rather than horse power.

Total Factor Productivity: Total Factor Productivity (also called multi-factor productivity) is a term used by economic professionals, including in the National Bureau of Economic Research, to describe the intangible element which contributes to the increasing productivity of an economy. That is, after accounting for all the inputs—an increase in labor quality, increase in capital intensity, and increase in the quality of capital—there are other factors which determine how efficiently these inputs are used. In analyzing the "Golden Age" of productivity of the United States, the economists pointed to infrastructure (the spread of electricity, for example) and technological innovation as the key determinants of TFP. For more information, see "Total Factor Productivity Growth in Historical Perspective" and Robert Gordon's *The Rise and Fall of American Growth*.

Wall Street: While Wall Street is often used simply as an epithet these days, I have tried to use it more precisely to describe the mega-banking community centered in Lower Manhattan (Wall Street), which dominates U.S. financial decisions, and maintains intimate relations with major international banking institutions, especially those in the City of London.

A PROPOSAL FOR A NEW HAMILTONIAN NATIONAL INFRASTRUCTURE BANK

DRAFT LEGISLATION
To Create a Bank of the United States for Infrastructure and Industry

SECTION I. FINDINGS AND PURPOSES

1. a) There is a broad consensus in the United States that we have reached a point where urgent steps must be taken to repair and upgrade our crumbling infrastructure. The nation needs a modern, 21st Century infrastructure and industrial platform, as is being constructed in many parts of the world. The American Society of Civil Engineers, International Association of Machinists and Aerospace Workers, U.S. Chamber of Commerce, and North America's Building Trades Unions estimate that a minimum of $3-5 trillion is needed to address the needs. A new national mission, like a Roosevelt New Deal or Kennedy Space Program, is needed to lift the nation

out of economic collapse, falling real wages, and cultural despair. Only a concerted effort comprised of federal appropriations, state and local programs, and a new National Bank for Infrastructure and Industry (hereafter known as "The Bank") can surmount this crisis.

2. b) Especially since the repeal of the Glass-Steagall Act and the emergence of interconnected "universal banks" of enormous size relative to the economy, the Federal Reserve Bank has pursued a policy resulting in near-zero investment in infrastructure and negligible capital spending in industry.

3. c) The establishment of The Bank operating as a commercial bank will be modeled on the approach of Treasury Secretary Alexander Hamilton to repurpose existing debt into useful projects. This was embodied in the First and Second Banks of the United States which generated remarkable increases in internal improvements, (infrastructure), and manufacturing. The Bank will utilize the most successful initiatives from those institutions, while balancing the needs and financial structures already in place. There is ample precedent for this. The application of Hamiltonian credit and bank policies has been extremely successful when used to advance production and increase productivity historically. The Lincoln National Banking Acts deployed this core approach to

positive effect when constructing the rail, canal, road building, and industrial expansion which built the nation. President Franklin Roosevelt's Reconstruction Finance Corporation, operating according to similar national bank principles, was instrumental in lifting the country out of the Great Depression and into a Golden Age of economic growth. The new Bank will restore the valid profit to the commercial banking system which arises from manufacturing, industry, increasing productivity of lands and soils, and the building of new, technologically advanced infrastructure which promotes these.

4. d) It is a purpose of the United States Congress in creating The Bank, to return to the level of progress of the United States "golden age of productivity," 1935-65, when multi-factor productivity advanced by 3-4% annually, in contrast to less than 0.5% annually over the past decade.

    (e) The Bank of the United States shall be chartered under the legislated means for carrying out the powers of Congress related to the purposes specified in Article I, Section 8 of the Constitution of the United States.

SECTION II. RESPONSIBILITIES AND AUTHORIZATIONS

(a) By this legislation, the Congress authorizes the creation of a public corporation to be called the National Bank of the United States for Infrastructure and Industry (The Bank) which is authorized to: provide credit for major national projects of infrastructure including surface transportation and ports, water management and supply, drought prevention, flood prevention and storm protection, electrical energy production and distribution, space exploration; make loans to agencies of the United States authorized for such projects; enter joint ventures with agencies of other nations to provide credit for major international projects of new infrastructure; provide credit to state and municipal capital projects by purchase of municipal bonds as issued; discount bank loans to businesses participating in such projects; and cooperate with the United States Export-Import Bank to provide trade credits to businesses engaged in international infrastructure projects.

(b) Projects funded by the Bank of the United States would expand Buy America provisions, protect and encourage the use of Project Labor Agreements, require the use of Davis–Bacon prevailing wage standards, ensure racial and gender equity in hiring, and guarantee investment in disadvantaged communities most in need, in urban and rural jurisdictions.

SECTION III. CAPITALIZATION AND CIRCULATING FUNDS OF THE BANK

(a) The Bank of the United States will be capitalized up to a maximum of $3 trillion by public holders of

(1) outstanding Treasury securities of three (3) years or greater maturity, and
(2) outstanding municipal bonds of Federal states or cities of five (5) years or greater maturity, who shall subscribe these securities as stock in the Bank, and shall receive in exchange, preferred shares in the Bank, callable during a period of 20 years only by the Bank, bearing fixed annual dividend to be determined by the Bank's Board of Directors, but not to be less than four (4)% per annum; dividend and redemption payments on the shares of the Bank to be guaranteed by the U.S. Treasury.

(b) The Treasury shall be an "on-call" subscriber to the Bank in an amount up to $100 billion in new issues of thirty (30)-year U.S. Treasury bonds, and shall receive the same amount in preferred shares in exchange.

(c) The Bank is hereby authorized to create deposits equal to the amount of each infrastructure loan made, subject to a total limit for all loans equal to the total capital subscribed to the Bank in the form of outstanding Treasury securities under Section III (a) (1) above. The Bank shall also accept deposits from individuals and corporations. It is authorized to receive repayment of loans into The Bank, and to re-circulate those funds into new or ongoing infrastructure projects.

(d) The Bank shall be authorized to receive U.S. government revenue deposits, specifically of the proceeds of the Federal tax on gasoline (the National Transportation Trust Fund), as a fund with which to pay the interest on its preferred stock. The bank shall also receive U.S. Government appropriations dedicated to service the interest on the preferred stock.

(e) The Bank shall receive into its circulating deposits, regular interest payments from the U.S. Treasury at intervals of one hundred and eighty (180) days on the outstanding Treasury securities which have been subscribed as capital in the Bank.

(f) State and municipal agencies which receive capital project support through purchase by the Bank of municipal capital bonds, shall be required to keep on deposit at the Bank, five (5) % of the proceeds of such bond purchases, until the completion and final commissioning of the project involved.

(g) The Bank shall be authorized to borrow from the discount windows of the Federal Reserve Banks for periods of up to one year, against state and municipal capital bonds which it has purchased.

(h) The Bank shall be authorized further to raise borrowed capital for its project investments from the public, from commercial banks and business corporations, and from investment funds, by issuing additional debenture bonds up to a total equal to its subscribed capital; these liabilities of the Bank shall have a guarantee from the United States Treasury; the bonds of the Bank shall be qualified for purchase by commercial banks operating under Glass-Steagall standards, and shall be discountable at Federal Reserve Banks.

(i) Subscribers to the capital of the Bank who are not U.S. citizens or U.S.-based institutions shall be non-voting shareholders.

SECTION IV. PRIVATE COMMERCIAL BANKS

(a) The Bank of the United States shall discount loans to participants in approved projects, made by commercial banks operating under Glass-Steagall standards of regulation. The rate of discounting of loans shall be determined by the Bank's Board of Directors, but shall not be less than 50%.

SECTION V: LOAN SPECIFICATIONS AND RESTRICTIONS

(a) The majority of loans and discounts made by the Bank should coincide in maturities with the time periods of anticipated profitability and projected useful life of the projects and new facilities financed with such loans and discounts.

(b) The Bank may make loans to companies involved in manufacturing related to the purposes of SECTION II for additional needs of capital expansion, where those companies can show that the additional capital cannot be obtained from local or regional private commercial banks.

(c) The Bank may extend the time for payment of a loan, through renewal, substitution of new obligations, or otherwise, with the maximum time for such renewal to be established by the Bank's Board of Directors. The Bank may make such further loans for completion of projects or additions, improvements, and extensions necessary for the proper functioning of the project, or which will increase assurance of the borrower to repay the entire loan or loans.

(d) The Bank may make loans which are initially in cooperation with other lending institutions, participating in such loans by up to 50%.

SECTION VI: BRANCHES

The Directors of the Bank shall establish an office of lending, discount, and deposit in each of the Federal Reserve Districts, and in any other state where Congress may require it by law.

SECTION VII: DIRECTORS

(a) There shall be 25 Directors of the Bank, appointed for terms of five (5) years by the President, subject to approval by the next annual general shareholders' meeting. The majority of the Directors shall be actively engaged in industrial or engineering activity or have had at least 15 years' experience in industry and/or infrastructure, to include at least two (2) representatives from the United States Army Corps of Engineers and at least two (2) representatives from the National Aeronautics and Space Administration and space industry, and three (3) officials of the AFL–CIO, including the Building and Construction Trades Department. The Board of Directors shall elect one of the Directors to be President of the Bank for a term of five (5) years and as necessary thereafter. The President shall be required to assemble a staff with experience in the commercial banking, engineering, heavy construction, and scientific fields, which he or she shall direct to assess the feasibility, productivity, and cost of investments.

(b) The Directors of the Bank, at their first meeting, shall decide on the schedule of their periodic meetings, and on a rotating Executive Committee which shall have authority to approve infrastructure projects, including international agreements for projects of particular importance, between regular meetings of the Board.

(c) The Bank shall receive from Congress an authorization of $100 million for the initial organization of the Bank's Directors and staff.

SECTION VIII: RESTRICTIONS

(a) The Bank shall not purchase public debt of the United States as issued, nor make any loan on the pledge thereof.

(b) The total amount of the debts which the Bank shall owe at any time may not exceed the capital stock of the Bank plus its deposits, unless the contracting of a greater debt shall have been authorized by an Act of Congress.

Primary Sources

The primary source for this book is the 26-volume collection of *The Papers of Alexander Hamilton*, edited by Harold C. Syrett & Jacob E. Cooke, and published by Columbia University Press beginning in 1961. This hard-copy collection was supplemented by the *Founders Online* digital collection run by the National Archives, and *The Federalist Papers*.

Additional primary sources were Adam Smith's *Wealth of Nations*; the writings of Mathew and Henry C. Carey; Friedrich List's *Outlines of American Political Economy*; the speeches of Abraham Lincoln; and the speeches and official addresses of President Franklin D. Roosevelt and John F. Kennedy, most of which are available online.

Secondary Sources

It is impossible to cite all the books and articles which I have read, and which have informed my thinking about Alexander Hamilton and his policies and legacy, over the past 40 years. Suffice it to say that

I have read both Hamilton's detractors (as in the recent book *How Alexander Hamilton Screwed Up America* by Brion McClanahan, published by Regnery History, 2017) and his fans in the course of my studies. What I list here are a few of the books and magazine articles which I found to be most useful to my research.

BOOKS

Bourgin, Frank, *The Great Challenge: The Myth of Laissez-Faire in the Early Republic*, Braziller press, New York, 1989.

Chaitkin, Anton, *Treason in America: From Aaron Burr to Averell Harriman*, Executive Intelligence Review, Washington, D.C., 1998.

Chernow, Ron, *Alexander Hamilton*, The Penguin Press, New York, 2004.

Fiske, John, *The Critical Period of American History, 1783-1789*, Houghton Mifflin Company, Boston and New York, 1888.

Hammond, Bray, *Banks and Politics in America, from the Revolution to the Civil War*, Princeton University Press, Princeton, N.J., 1957.

Knott, Stephen E. & Williams, Tony, *Washington and Hamilton: The Alliance That Forged America*, Sourcebooks, Inc., Naperville, Illinois, 2015.

Liebig, Michael, ed. *Friedrich List, Outlines of American Political Economy*, Dr. Böttiger Verlags-GmbH, Wiesbaden, Germany, 1992.

McDonald, Forrest, *Alexander Hamilton, A Biography*, W.W. Norton & Company, New York, 1979.

McDonald, Forrest, *E Pluribus Unum: the formation of the American Republic, 1776-1790*, Liberty Fund, Indianapolis, 1965.

Salisbury, Allen, *The Civil War and the American System: America's Battle with Britain 1860-1876*, Executive Intelligence Review, Washington, D.C., 1992.

Spannaus, Nancy & White, Christopher, eds. *The Political Economy of the American Revolution*, Executive Intelligence Review, Washington, D.C., 1996.

ARTICLES

One of the most insightful articles on Hamilton's economic orientation was Donald F. Swanson's "Origins of Hamilton's Fiscal Policies," University of Florida Monographs, *Social Sciences*, No. 17, Winter 1963, *passim*.

Readers may note that the majority of the articles cited in my text were originally published by the U.S. newsweekly *Executive Intelligence Review*, which was edited in various capacities by the author for many decades up until 2015. During much of that period, the magazine was heavily devoted to publishing unique historical research on the American System, making information buried in academic journals and archives available to the general public. This author played an initiating role in this work, and participated in the research for, and edited, many of these articles.

One of the most fruitful studies was contained in the January 3, 1992 edition of *EIR*, entitled "200 Years Since Hamilton's Report on Manufactures." That issue featured articles and excerpts of original sources demonstrating Hamilton's influence in American economic development, and that of Russia, Japan, Germany, and other nations. I have cited several of those articles, which shed extraordinary light on an otherwise-hidden story of Hamilton's intellectual influence.

Another comprehensive, multi-article feature appeared in the June 22, 2012 edition of *Executive Intelligence Review,* under the title "Why the Empire Destroyed the Second National Bank."

Other major *EIR* studies I found invaluable were:

Chaitkin, Anton, "How Carey and Bismarck Transformed Germany," *Executive Intelligence Review,* April 28, 2006.

Freeman, Richard, "Then and Now: Why FDR's Explosive 1933-1945 Recovery Worked," *Executive Intelligence Review,* April 26, May 3, and May 10, 2002 editions.

Kirsch, Michael, "The Credit System vs. Speculation: Nicholas Biddle and the 2nd Bank of the United States," *Executive Intelligence Review,* July 20, 2012.

Kirsch, Michael, "How Andrew Jackson Destroyed the United States," *Executive Intelligence Review,* Dec. 14, 2012.

(Note: Since Alexander Hamilton's name appears on virtually every page of this book, it is not included in the index.)

CPSIA information can be obtained
at www.ICGtesting.com
Printed in the USA
LVHW092004201220
674700LV00023B/330

9 781532 067549